To The Carl A. Rudisill Library -
Lenoir Rhyne College,

...much mukluk,

*[signature]*

ketchikan, Alaska
1972

917.98
W56h

80977

DATE DUE

| | | | | | | | | | | |
|---|---|---|---|---|---|---|---|---|---|---|
| Apr22 '75 | | | | | | | | | | |
| May13 '75 | | | | | | | | | | |
| Oct 2 '75 | | | | | | | | | | |
| Oct16 '75 | | | | | | | | | | |
| Apr 7  78 | | | | | | | | | | |
| Mar2  '8 | | | | | | | | | | |
| Mar25 '8 | | | | | | | | | | |

**FIRST EDITION**
10,000 Copies

Distributed in Alaska by **GORDON GODFRED & ASSOCIATES,** 219 East 51st Avenue, Anchorage, Alaska 99503 to Gift Shops

Published by **MARK WHEELER/PUBLISHER,** 405 Dock Street, Ketchikan, Alaska 99901

**MAIL ORDERS** should be directed to **THE VOYAGEUR BOOK SHOP,** 405 Dock Street, Ketchikan, Alaska 99901

# half baked alaska

## by Mark Wheeler

Library of Congress Catalog Number 74-185755

917.98
W56h

80977
November 1972

Printed in Canada by
EVERGREEN PRESS LIMITED
Vancouver, B.C.

# FOREWORD

Somebody once said, "Find a need and fill it." If the author of this challenge could have foreseen my interpretation, he might not have ventured the thought.

One need in Alaska, it seems to me, is to confirm all the misconceptions about Uncle Sam's Attic. Every cold nose knows there is currently an abundance of these misconceptions and, therefore, there is naturally an obvious need for more.

For justice to be done, the laws of supply and demand are on trial here and this volume is designed to satisfy both sides.

To the casual traveler Alaska smacks of foreign country. Very nice folks, obviously from elsewhere, come to Alaska almost daily. The poor dears get hopelessly lost among the language, the scenery, and the quality of the Alaskan life. Most do not know the difference between a whale, or to wail; or a vein, a vane, or to be vain. Some need to be guided to differentiate when someone is said to be "sealing" whether he is hunting seals or licking envelopes.

Hopefully all this jumbled jargon will become more or less vague and all the misconceptions about the Great Land will be further misunderstood after you help yourself to this generous portion of Half Baked Alaska.

Aloha, Mark Wheeler

MANY OF THE IDEAS FOR THIS BOOK FIRST APPEARED IN MY MONTHLY CARTOON PAGE IN THE "NEW ALASKAN" A PRETTY LIVELY NEWSPAPER IN SOUTHEASTERN ALASKA!

# DEDICATION

Half Baked Alaska is a labor of love not only for an occasional yuk but for all Alaska and Alaskans. The visitor will find Alaskans (most everywhere, there) have an almost ferocious pride in their state and share a great spirit which should be an example to the rest of the country.

This book is dedicated to all the great folks of Alaska overall and specifically to Bob Briant who sold my watercolors when he owned The Voyageur Book Shop in Ketchikan, who gave me my start in Alaska, and to Bob Pickrell, publisher of "The New Alaskan" who publishes my cartoons, cover art, stories, and ads in his lively newspaper which has contributed tremendously to my young career in Alaska.

Further dedication is to the hapless souls who believe one (or more) word of this book to be true.

And now a note of faith: It is hoped that not too much of the material in this book will raise too much cain with you but if it does, I have faith that you will let me know. I plan to write a couple more books on Alaska and I need all the ideas I can get.

I wish also to extend a very special note of thanks to Mr. and Mrs. Ed Magden of Ketchikan without whose help the presses would not have rolled.

*Muck Mukluk*

## OTHER STUFF YOU OUGHT'A KNOW

Alaska is a very big place (586,412 square miles at high tide) and has just about one person for every two square miles. The proportion of funny things happening per capita has to be the highest in the country. The problem is all the funny things are unrelated to funny things that happen anywhere else.

Half Baked Alaska is designed to aid the casual traveler (and the native) in getting around the Great Land and not appear or sound too foolish. You can take this book along when you travel, or mail it to folks you don't like, or relatives who are coming to Alaska, or you can put butter between the pages and use it for a sandwich, or you can save it to warm a chilly night (put it in a 350° oven for 30 minutes, wrap it in a clean beach towel and put it in your bed) or you can line your bird cage with the 160 pages for an undetermined number of days (depending on the size of your bird).

You should know too that there were at least three distinct sources for the material in this book. These sources were: (1) Reliable, (2) Unreliable, and (3) Drunk.

**Reliable Source:** For the most part these are sources which a lack of time prevented me from confirming what they told me and they had no reason to fib to me at the moment.

**Unreliable Source:** These are primarily people (though not all were) who seemed to be suffering the varied effects of Gold Fever (Klondikeitus), Buck Fever (Sixpointism) or Cabin Fever (Oneroomatism).

**Drunk Sources:** Some of these were people who, at the time, were holding varied colored bottles and canning jars at various angles to their mouths, draining them of their strange smelling contents. One was a bear who was suspected of fueling on fermented huckleberries.

7

For the sake of sanity I have omitted labeling each individual story so that you can make up neat games about which story came from which source and so that one glassy-eyed bear with an aching head and huckleberries on his breath will feel no malice towards me.

Half Baked Alaska has no chapters simply because the nature of the state defies categorizing. Included however is a glossary of terms that the reader will need in his wanderings. Almost everyone in Alaska has a different idea of what these words mean but none of them match mine.

After considerable proofreading it is hoped that this volume is free from any specific facts, specific dates, or specifically anything else void of humor.

What ever you do, remember the advice of the Sourdough Philosopher who said, "Hold all truths up to the light and notice how thin many are. . ."

8

The goofy-looking kid in the picture above is none other than the author and publisher and thinker-upper of this whole volume, which he did while painting watercolors . . . his name is . . . a . . .

"Cynthia will be right down . . . she just has to finish skinning out her moose."

MARK WHEELER

9

**HOW To KNOW iF YOU COULD EVER BECOME A REAL ALASKAN:**

YOU COULD IF YOU GET MOST OF THE STUFF IN THIS BOOK.
YOU COULD NOT (PROBABLY) IF YOU:
1. DON'T LIKE THE OUTDOORS.
2. DON'T LIKE RUGGED PEOPLE.
3. NEED LOTS OF WARM, DRY, WEATHER.
4. DON'T LIKE SCENERY.
5. WORK FROM SUN UP TO SUN DOWN.
6. ARE TOO FUSSY.

## RUGGED PEOPLE

People have to be pretty rugged to survive in Alaska. The average teenager (young person) can hit, run, pitch, bat, and catch a moose all by him (or her) self. Parents teach their young basic lessons in either woodsmanship or snowmanship before they go to school because they'll need to know it to get to the schoolhouse. The kids in Florida don't get that kind of learning.

## TAXES

Alaska has fewer people per square mile than anywhere else in the U.S.A. Every resident of the state can call about two square miles of land his own. If that were actually possible just remember downtown Anchorage is mine.

With so few people (300,000) and so much land (586,412 square miles) it is pretty tough to build a road, school, city hall or dog pound for $300,000 and that is a buck out of everybody.

Construction costs are half a budget higher and the building season is shorter than most places so it takes a lot of taxes to pay for it all.

All these taxes make assessors less than friends of the people. Luckily for the homeowner houses can be disguised as boats, igloos, hollowed logs, caves, and lean-tos, which are very hard to assess as homes. Lucky too for the dogs who can make a meal out of an assessor on a moment's notice.

10

*"If a very official looking guy in a car marked **'Assessor'** shows up, you tear his leg off!"*

11

*"We can certainly count our blessings serving here . . . all this rain . . . so few golf courses . . . no long Sunday drives . . ."*

MARK WHEELER

12

# RELIGION

If there is anything in Alaska to hold in reverence it certainly should be religion. Alaska has made its devotions a wide variety of ways. The Russians built a whole big bunch of churches, most of them Russian Orthodox. Not everyone thought the Russians were that orthodox but the Russians had an ulterior motive.

In those days Alexander Baranof and his Rag Time Band were out grabbing sea otters which were sold, much to the dismay of the otters themselves.

Baranof and his Banditos were making so much bread (unleavened) in the form of gold they decided they had better make candlesticks or something so they could make tremendous contributions to the church which they could take off their income taxes.

The plan worked great for everyone except the sea otters who all caught a death of cold without their pelts.

The Russians were up to other tricks too. Sitka was one of them. The Russians always seemed to build their churches in places with names that defied pronunciation. Places like Eklutna and Unalaska. The natives wouldn't tell the Russians how to say or spell the name so they couldn't tell other Russians about the place. Lucky for the Russians they couldn't speak Aleut or Eskimo or Sitkanese so after 1867 they left town after the sheriff told them he would run them out on a rail . . . if he could find a rail.

Today many modern religions are practiced in Alaska. In Barrow they vary the practice of Baptism in the winter when it's pretty tough to get baptised in ice, and in Ketchikan they just bless the rain and hold the service outdoors. So far they've never had a lack of cooperation from the weather.

All in all Alaska is said to be rather divine.

## THE ELEMENTS

Among the elements in Alaska can be found Bad Weather, Very Bad Weather, Plutonium, Fog, and Right Front (also known as a heating element or "burner"). To protect yourself against all of these you need adequate clothing.

Seal skin coats have now been discovered to be waterproof (something the seals have known for years), and other clothes are made from other stuff. Parts of sea animals (mammals, to be correct) are used to make all varieties of inside and outside wearing apparel.

One thing to remember before you try on a wolf fur parka, for example, is to make sure the wolf is not still in it too.

"UP HERE WE DON'T COUNT THE YEARS WE'VE BEEN HERE...JUST THE WINTERS!"

## PARKA

The garment known as a parka is a most ingenious member of the Alaskan wardrobe. Parkas are made from a variety of animal skins, canvas, and other heavy materials. Virtually no parkas are made of chiffon, organza, or tricot.

By the time a parka gets all put together (by a "parkor," something like a tailor) a parka might add a third again as much weight as the wearer.

In fact when someone goes out on snowshoes he must first calculate the weight of the parka, plus his own weight plus the weight of his pack and then determine how many square inches of snowshoe surface he needs to keep from sinking into the snow. A missed computation or calculation could result in a misfortune not unlike that of the *Titanic*. To be off either way is dangerous. Too heavy and he'll sink, too light and his feet won't touch the ground.

14

*"With everybody wearing 25 pound parkas, building a coat rack is no easy job!"*

MARK WHEELER

15

HOW TO SPOT AN ALASKAN:

THE AVERAGE ALASKAN IS ABOUT 28 YEARS OLD. MORE ARE MALE THAN ANYTHING ELSE...

- FRIENDLY DISPOSITION

- USUALLY MANY MUSCLES (ON BOTH MEN & WOMEN) FROM ALL THE HARD WORK ALASKANS DO...

NOSE USUALLY COLD OR AT LEAST CHILLED.

- KNOWN TO DRINK A BIT...

- CITIZEN OF U.S.A.

- HARD WORKER

- MIGHT RESENT GOVERNMENT INTERVENTION SOMETIMES

- OVERALL SENSE OF INTENSE PRIDE IN ALASKA...
- LOVES TO FLY
- GOOD OUTDOORSMAN
- TAX PAYER

SHARP EYE OUT FOR WEATHER...

EAR TUNED FOR BELLOWING MOOSE...

- WILL POSE

- SUFFERS FROM BUCK FEVER IN FALL

- HIGH INCOME

- NOT AFRAID OF RAIN OR SNOW

- IN SOUTH-EASTERN WEARS BROWN RUBBER BOOTS

- PIONEER SPIRIT

- MAN'S MAN

- STRONG

HANDS SHOWING EITHER SIZE OF FISH CAUGHT OR SIZE OF MOSQUITOES...

MARK WHEELER

16

## ALASKANS

To be classified as a real honest-to-goodness native-born Alaskan is a real rarity because so few Alaskans are. Most Alaskans were born some place other than Alaska and other places as well. Very few tourists can call themselves Alaskans except those who were born in Juneau but are now visiting Douglas. Those are Alaskan Tourists touring Alaska. Other tourists are known as "foreigners" or "Texans" and a tour bus manager I know calls them "Pilgrims."

*Alaskan: *CAN BE: NATIVE, INDIAN, ALEUT, ESKIMO, RESIDENT...

"HE SAYS THIS IS ALASKA... HE MUST BE AN ALASKAN... HE SURE LOOKS FOREIGN..."

## ALASKAN HISTORY

The Eleventh Edition of the *Encyclopaedia Britannica*, printed in 1911, states on page 476:
"The white population is extremely mobile, and few towns have an assured or definite future. The prosperity of the mining towns of the interior is dependent on the fickle fortune of the gold-fields, for which they are the distributing points. Sitka, Juneau (the capital) and Douglas, both centres of a rich mining district, Skagway, shipping point for freight for the Klondike country, and St. Michael, the ocean port for freighting up the Yukon, are the only towns apparently assured of a prosperous future. Wrangell (formerly Fort St. Dionysius, Fort Stikine and Fort Wrangell), founded in 1833, is a dilapidated and torpid little village, of some interest in Alaskan history, and of temporary importance from 1874 to 1877 as the gateway to the Cassiar Mines in British Columbia. Its inhabitants are chiefly Tlingit Indians."

ALASKA HISTORY NOTE: THE STATE ACTUALLY GOT ITS NAME FROM SENATOR CHARLES SUMNER IN 1867

17

"This must be the famous **Alaska Marine Highway!**"

# AMERICANS

Some folks, proud of heritage and roots and all that, believe the only true Americans are the Indians. When one boasts of being "100 per cent American" the obvious retort is, "which tribe?" This brings us to a very basic question: What were Alaskans before they became Americans?

By way of answer you might have to ask yet another question: Were Indians Indians before they became Americans?

Ah . . . there lies the nut. Indians were a very peaceful folk who were maize-growing, pipe-smoking pals before Christopher Columbus sailed along. As we all know, young Chris, thinking he had bumped into India, proclaimed all to be Indians. But when that jolly Dane, Vitus Bering, who was sporting a fur coat long before it was fashionable for men of stable repute to wear a fur, discovered Alaska he didn't have the slightest idea what to call the folks he dis-

covered. In fact he was having second thoughts about being there in the first place.

As we all know by now, old Vitus must have stood in pretty good stead among his discover-ees (those are folks what's been discovered) because old Mr. Bering not only forced his will on the natives but gave them a new collective name too.

The natives, in turn, changed the lore of Alaska. The night after Vitus left for good the natives were heard singing in unison "Dane'ta gonna be lore no more no more. . ."

AMERICANS:

"BACK IN AMERICA DO YOU STILL HAVE COWBOYS?"

19

WHaT To see & Do ABove THe ARcTic CiRcLe iN ALaska:

VISIT FORT YUKON — EXPERIENCE THE WEATHER

STUDY ARCTIC LIFE · HUNT · FISH · EAT · WEAR MUK-LUKS · HELLO DAN! VISIT BARROW

VISIT KoTZeBUE AND DON'T BE BLUE! SEE: THE KING-ISLAND ESKIMO DANCERS · IVORY BLANKET TOSS BUMP INTO

HELLO ALASKA AIRLINES! POST NO BILLS HUNT WHALES · GET A SEAL CARVING · OOMIAK THE ARCTIC CIRCLE!

THE AIRPORT FOR PRUD-HOE BAY HELLO ARCO! VISIT DEADHORSE

VISIT THE SCHWATKA MOUNTAINS HUNT · FISH · LOOK · SEE · HEAR · SMELL · TASTE · LIVE

SEE BROOK RANGE

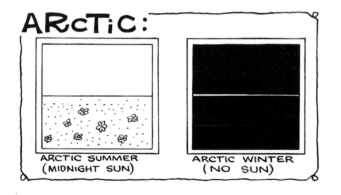

ARcTic:

ARCTIC SUMMER (MIDNIGHT SUN)

ARCTIC WINTER (NO SUN)

## ARCTIC

Kotzebue, Alaska, is above the Arctic Circle. Nobody can see the forest for the tree there. That's all there is in Kotzebue National Forest. One very brave little struggling example of a tree. When from all the seeds planted, only one tree grew, a plan to turn the area into a forest had to abandoned. After all who has ever heard of a forest with only one tree?

20

*"Somehow these vending machines take a lot of fun out of Arctic life. . ."*

21

WHAT TO DO WITH A BILLIKIN AFTER YOU BUY ONE...

PUT IT ON THE MANTEL.
CARRY IT IN YOUR POCKET.
MAKE A TIE TAC.
BUY TWO AND MAKE CUFF LINKS.
MAKE A KEY FOB.
USE AS A MANNEQUIN.
MAKE INTO EARRINGS.
MAKE A WATCHBAND.

BILLIKIN:

"A FRIEND OF MINE RUBBED THE TUMMY OF A BILLIKIN BUT IT WAS REALLY JUST A GUY DRESSED THAT WAY..."

## BILLIKIN

The billikin is a neat little character which is supposed to have all kinds of super magical powers. When one acquires a billikin he should receive the little saying that goes with the critter. The saying is: "As a blues chaser, I'm a honey; whenever you're sad just rub my tummy."

Whether the magic really works or not nobody knows.

## ESKIMOS ORDERING

Eskimos love to order things from the mail-order places. Nobody knows what they do with some of it, but at least by ordering something they are assured of getting a new catalog and we have a pretty good idea what they do with it. Reading matter is sometimes hard to come by in the far north but the mail always gets through. So anything the mailman can carry gets ordered and many times the item ordered is bigger than the post office.

22

MARK WHEELER

"I understand that salesman is Number One in his company!"

## ALASKA

Alaska varies greatly in size at various times of the day. This is because of the tides. At low tide Alaska is about two and one half times bigger than Texas plus the areas covered by downtown Denver, New Castle County, Delaware, Yankee Stadium, and the hangar deck of the aircraft carrier U.S.S. *Midway.*

At high tide Alaska is only two and a half times bigger than Texas but hopes that nobody got caught in the tide in those other places, especially Denver.

Some towns in Alaska, especially seacoast towns, have rules stating that if a cab driver picks up a fare who wants to go to the docks, and who appears to be intoxicated, the driver has to escort the passenger to water level. The reason is sometimes the tide will drop 35′ while the man has been "uptown" and he may fall down the gangway and injure himself or even drown. The tide can drop that far in a couple of hours.

24

## VITUS BERING

Vitus Bering the Dane turned out to be a pretty Great Dane after all. In Denmark (where virtually 100% of all Danes come from) he couldn't decide whether he should spell his name *Behring* or *Bering* but finally took the latter when his father gave him a matched set of luggage with the name gold-stamped that way.

Peter the Great, who had learned Russia had a Navy, sent young Vitus to see (and to sea) if Asia was connected to America. Peter had hoped to exchange color post cards with George Washington but discovered he wasn't to be born until seven years later, much less the father of anything.

Bering had a very nice voyage but lost his hearing and his Vitamin C and found he had scurvy. He died in 1741 at the age of 61, which made him ineligible for his pension.

But when the naming crew from the Post Office and the Geodetic Department came around they named a village, an island, a sea, and a glacier as well as a bunch of other places after him. All those places are today bearing Bering.

CITY 78' FEET UP (IN THE CLOUDS)

THE TIDE IS OUT

MOUNTAIN WHARF CLIMBING GEAR FOR RENT ☆
CHARGE CARDS WELCOME.
NO DEPOSIT • LOW MILEAGE CHARGE!

Rates ☆
10 STEPS $1.50
20 STEPS $2.50
30 STEPS $10.00

RENT IT HERE... LEAVE IT THERE!

MARK WHEELER

"Look pal, you've got to decide who is smarter, you or the fish . . . you can't let 'em walk all over ya . . . ya can't let 'em get the upper hand . . . and you had better not tell them I'm coming to get 'em again!"

26

## STATE FISH

The State Fish is the King Salmon. Story has it the salmon thinks the letter "L" in his name, since it isn't pronounced, is quite wasteful. Since the salmon is such an important part of the Alaskan economy the word "Salmon" appears in all kinds of government reports, on millions of labels on cans, and is printed lots of other places. Each little letter "L" takes a certain amount of ink to print and when you multiply that amount of ink by the umpteentrillions, it adds up to a lot of money wasted.

While the salmon are out working so hard making money for a lot of folks, they resent some of that money being wasted on something that isn't even used, and they don't even need.

SALMON PROVIDE A LOT OF NET INCOME FOR FISHERMEN IN ALASKA

MARK WHEELER

27

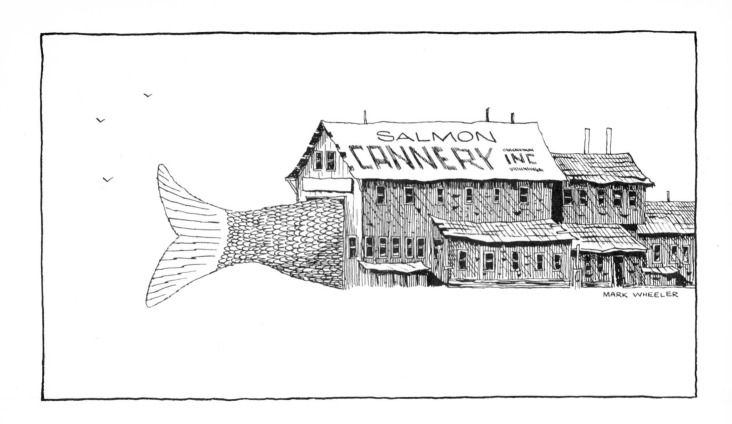

SALMON CANNERY INC

MARK WHEELER

## CANNERIES

The problem of what to do with all the fish everyone catches in Alaska was studied for years. One plan was to run ads all over the country with a coupon that you could use to mail back to get a salmon, postage paid. The postmaster in Hot Bluff, Texas opposed the plan saying, "It stinks."

Then one day a fisherman, using worms for bait which he carried in a can, ran out of worms after he had caught a few very small fish. He didn't want to just put the fish in his pocket, so he put them in the can. For a lid he used one of his wife's sourdough biscuits, on which he had earlier broken a tooth.

The can had a piece of paper wrapped around it that said, "Fish Food" but thinking that was redundant he crossed out the word "Food" and took it home. Many months later his wife found the can perfectly preserved because she had put too much salt in the biscuit in the first place. Thus was the beginning of the canning business.

## FISH

Some of the fresh water fish don't like the salt water fish and their beefs are widely known in Alaska. The salt water fish have greater freedom by the very fact that there is more salt water in which to swim around. The only areas the fresh water fish can use are scattered lakes and streams with limited scenery but the salt water fish can go where ever they want.

This is pretty much a jurisdictional battle with really no possible winner. The main problem seems to be that the fresh water fish and the salt water fish have had a hard time getting together on neutral ground to negotiate.

## JOBLESS FISH

Salmon work very hard at what they do best. They swim around, entertain tourists, provide nice dinners, and adorn the fronts of menus and mantels. But now they're mad. Some seasons are worse than others but the jobless rate remains high. Just at the peak of their careers a lot of them seem to get themselves canned.

29

*"Ethel, for the last time there are no snakes in Alaska and nothing can hurt you, so just go to sleep . . ."*

MARK WHEELER

30

## SPRING

Spring in Alaska reveals all varieties of new life. Break-up is a term that refers to the melting and eventual break-up of ice in the rivers of the north.

It also means the break-up of many a bear's happy home, as his spring alarm goes off and he comes out of his bedroom and starts looking for berries, fish, and various flavors of hunters to eat.

The whole of life is a break-up too as booze sales go down, bikini sales go up and, like in Fairbanks for example, the temperature is climbing from a winter low of -50° or less up to a summer high of 90° plus. That breaks up everybody.

Spring is also when the squabble rate goes down as does the booze consumption rate. The squabble rate is the rate at which people are hauled to jail and to court to settle family beefs. Being penned up by the weather does it.

31

"If we do get lost, we'll just shoot something out of season and a game warden will be here in less than a minute!"

MARK WHEELER

32

## BUCK FEVER (Sixpointism)

Every year certain people, mainly men, fall victim to a strange malady known commonly as "Buck Fever." The symptoms are glazed eyes, listless moping about the house, incoherent speech and constant mumbling using words like "buck," "eight point," "over the ridge," "shale slide," "in the clearing," "out of range," and "I bagged it."

There is only one remedy known. Eight out of ten Wrangell doctors recommend at least one week in the brush. One week of total isolation from any one or all of the kids, bills, domestic squabbles, and/or wife mate (if the wife also gets buck fever, take her along).

## BUCK PASSING

There is another type of buck involved in this buck fever syndrome too. It's the kind of buck that is six inches long, has numbers in its corners, has a green back, and is made of paper.

It takes a lot of these bucks to get the other bucks. Both types can be elusive but the paper ones are easier to fold into your wallet.

Also if you are out purchasing something the second type of bucks are more adaptable to being stored in a cash register, especially in volume.

Be sure you know which kind of bucks you are going to use to get the other kind of bucks.

BUCK FEVER: (SIXPOINTISM)

ASK ANY DEER HUNTER WHAT IT MEANS...

33

*"Fly up and tell the bears they ain't seen nothin' yet ..."*

MARK WHEELER

34

## BUSH PILOTS

Opposite of what mental picture "Bush Pilot" forms in your mind, such an aviator doesn't fly around in a shrub or tree. Bush Pilots are legendary in Alaska and whole big volumes have been issued about them.

One such pilot was old Sopwith Roose who flew the famous amphibious craft known as a "goose." Sopwith flew his trusty craft all over Alaska and would carry any variety of cargo.

One flying day Roose was asked to carry a moose on his goose. Roose agreed but when the moose got to the terminal Roose could readily see that the moose was intoxicated. Roose wasn't about to ferry a juiced moose on his goose.

## FLYING

A lot of Alaskans are up in the air about . . . flying, especially if they live on an island.

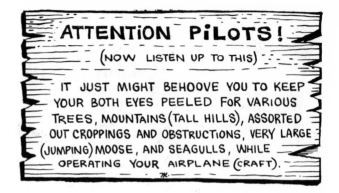

ATTENTION PILOTS! (NOW LISTEN UP TO THIS)

IT JUST MIGHT BEHOOVE YOU TO KEEP YOUR BOTH EYES PEELED FOR VARIOUS TREES, MOUNTAINS (TALL HILLS), ASSORTED OUT CROPPINGS AND OBSTRUCTIONS, VERY LARGE (JUMPING) MOOSE, AND SEAGULLS, WHILE OPERATING YOUR AIRPLANE (CRAFT).

BUSH PILOT:

SOMEONE WHO HAS THE ABILITY TO MAKE A SHRUB OR TREE TRAVEL GREAT DISTANCES WITHOUT EVER TOUCHING THE GROUND, AND TO CARRY PASSENGERS RIGHT ALONG WITH IT. (SOME BUSH PILOTS WORK FOR "TRUNK" AIR SERVICES...)

*"Terry over at the flying service said I could fly with him and be his navigator. . ."*

MARK WHEELER

36

## MORE ON FLYING

As we know, one of the best ways to get around Alaska is to fly, which is something the birds have known a lot longer than the people have. The big jets go lots of places these days but since nobody has come up with an amphibious 707 yet, the little planes (with floats or skis) are still quite popular.

*Very few airplanes have cow catchers.*

## ALASKA RAILROAD

The Alaska Railroad is quite a rig. It goes from Fairbanks to Seward which is about 463 miles. A plan to extend the railroad to Kodiak was abandoned when Kodiak was discovered to be on an island some distance from the mainland.

THE ALASKA RAILROAD ONCE TRIED TO CUT EXPENSES BY 50% BY HAVING THEIR TRAINS JUST RUN ON <u>ONE RAIL</u>...

WHAT THE CARS ON THE ALASKA RAILROAD LOOK LIKE...
NOTE: IF THIS TRAIN PASSES YOU WHILE YOU ARE IN KETCHIKAN OR BARROW PLEASE CALL THE MISSING TRAINS BUREAU BECAUSE IT'S ONLY SUPPOSED TO GO FROM SEWARD TO FAIRBANKS.

CRABOOSE - GONDOLA CAR - BAUXCAR - REFRIGERATED · FLAT CAR - COAL CAR · ENGINE WITH
(TO HAUL OLD CRABS)          (TO HAUL BAUXITE)   CAR                    (VERY TENDER) MOOSE CATCHER
THE RAILROAD THUMPS A MOOSE QUITE OFTEN · THEY GIVE THE MEAT TO ORPHANAGES AND THE NEEDY.

37

# WHY a NaTioNaL BiRD?

— A REALLY DUMB (BUT ORIGINAL) POEM —

THE BALD EAGLE
LOOKS NOTHING LIKE A BEAGLE;
SO WHAT GOOD DOES IT DO, YOU ASK,
SIT IN THE SUN THE DAY TO BASK?

NOT IN ALASKA, YOU SAY, ALL THAT RAIN;
THEN WHY AN EAGLE SAID TO BE SO VAIN?
WHY NOT A COW OR A MOOSE
OR BEAVER, MUSK OX, OR GOOSE?

BUT WAIT, A GOOSE IS A BIRD
THOUGHT NATIONALLY TO BE ABSURD,
BUT JUST AS A BIRD SOARS SO IDEALLY,
EAGLES HAVE DONE SO QUITE SURREALLY.

BEING FIERCE AND STRONG IS THE EAGLES WAY
OF SHOWING US HOW TO LIVE BETTER EACH DAY.
SO AN EAGLE IT IS, OUR NATIONAL BIRD
NOT CARING AT ALL, EVEN IF IT IS ABSURD.

THIS POEM (SIC) SHOULD BE CAST IN BRONZE JUST LIKE HIGH FLAOOTIN' THINGS REAL POLITICIANS SAY ALL THE TIME AND THEN HANG 'EM SOMEWHERE...

MARK WHEELER

## EAGLES

While in Alaska you might spot a living example of our National Bird (whom you'll remember from our money years ago). The Bald Eagle is getting kind of scarce. Actually eagles themselves aren't so scarce but bald eagles are.

To have little bald eagles it takes the usual combination of a male and a female eagle. But very few female eagles wanted to be seen with any chrome-domed bald eagles, what with men's toupees and hair stylists and what have you these days.

The female eagles told the male bald eagles to march right downtown and at least buy a hat or something but so far the males have refused. They say if the females get that ruffled about their heads then what'll be next?

38

*"Harold! Such a way you talk about our National Bird!"*

MARK WHEELER

*"You could save yourself a lot of work by hiring me to deliver all the catalogs and magazines. . ."*

40

## FLYOVERS

Most mail in Alaska goes air-mail. The reason for this is, naturally, speed. In Southeastern, for example, most towns are small and for the seasoned pilot, they are just a hop, skip, and a jump apart from each other. Unfortunately, the passengers (if there are any) make some of the same hops, skips, and jumps as the plane and the mail.

Also in Southeastern the weather is so bad many times that the residents suffer what is known as a "fly-over." That is the weather is so bad the planes can't land. No planes means no mail. Relief checks fly over, Mail order catalogs fly over, and so do the bills. Alaskans say so what? The only priority item is the mail order catalogs which are more useful than the other mail Alaskans get. In fact Alaskans get many times more mail than they send out, which makes all the mailmen 50% happier than all other mailmen.

(HERE IS A MINI-LETTER YOU CAN FILL-IN BEFORE YOU MAIL THIS BOOK TO YOUR MORE SNOOTY FRIENDS)

GREETINGS from ALASKA

Dear_____ :

Golly, Alaska sure is_____! My igloo is very_____ and, with my parka (that's like a coat), I'm quite _____. Yesterday I almost got eaten by a_____! I was just out gathering_____ when all of a sudden this big old_____ started after me! The_____ says I'll get out in two or 3 months. It sure is hard to write with 4 fingers gone though! More_____! Aloha_____

41

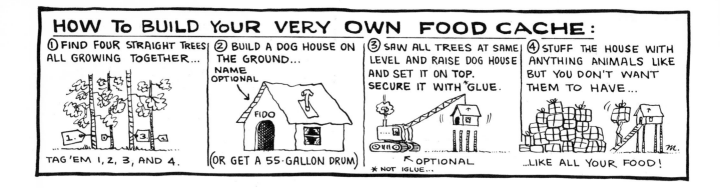

**HOW To BUILD YoUR VERY OWN FOOD CACHE:**

① FIND FOUR STRAIGHT TREES ALL GROWING TOGETHER... TAG 'EM 1, 2, 3, AND 4.

② BUILD A DOG HOUSE ON THE GROUND... NAME OPTIONAL. FIDO (OR GET A 55-GALLON DRUM)

③ SAW ALL TREES AT SAME LEVEL AND RAISE DOG HOUSE AND SET IT ON TOP. SECURE IT WITH *GLUE. ↖ OPTIONAL. * NOT IGLUE...

④ STUFF THE HOUSE WITH ANYTHING ANIMALS LIKE BUT YOU DON'T WANT THEM TO HAVE... ...LIKE ALL YOUR FOOD!

## CACHE

What looks like a house built before the tide went out is known as a "cache." Food stuffs and other stuff are stored in them. In the winter they act as a refrigerator and in the summer as any other house built on stilts. They are built higher than the animals in the area so the animals can't get at what's inside. Not a bad idea except when it snows. . .

**cache:** "CACHE" IS FOUND IN A VARIETY OF FORMS AND IS SOMETIMES INDICATED BY THE SYMBOL "$." YOU NEED A PRETTY GOOD SIZED ROLL OF IT TO TRAVEL AROUND IN ALASKA.

42

"I wonder what kind of a dog lives in a house like that?"

MARK WHEELER

43

## CHiLL FaCToR :

IN MEXICO, THE RATIO OF CHILI BEANS TO SPICES AND PEPPERS WHEN ALL ARE INGREDIENTS OF A KIND OF THICK, LUMPY SOUP MOST COMMONLY CALLED "WATCHITHOTSTUFFCOMINGTHROUGH."

*Alaska's highest recorded temperature: 100°*

**WHY YOU SHOULD NOT GET Too EXCiTED oveR CHiLL FACTOR :**

CHiLL FACTOR:
X + W.S ÷ X4
2 -+ ½ × 7:1
+ 4 ÷ WS · 1:T
/73 : 1½ =
± 80°

THE ONLY TIME CHILL FACTOR IS IMPORTANT IS WHEN YOU ARE OUT-OF-DOORS. AS FAR AS WIND CHILL GOES, THE SAME GOES. CONVERSELY THE REVERSE HOLDS... THAT IS, WITH NO WIND THERE CAN BE SIMPLY LOW TEMPERATURES WHICH DON'T INVOLVE ANY OF THE ABOVE.

44

## CHILL FACTOR

One rule of thumb to check chill factor is to lick it (your thumb) and hold it up in the breeze. If it immediately turns white, cracks and falls off, you can surmise the weather, wind, and temperature have a tendency to be rather nasty at the time.

Chill factor is the cooling effect of the wind compounded by low temperatures.

In Mexico, Chill Factor has a completely different meaning. There, Chill Factor has to do with the ratio of beans and Chilly Peppers brewed up in a kind of lumpy soup.

Chill Factor is also known as "Wind Chill," "Wind Factor" and a few other synonyms we won't go into.

From surveys we've learned it doesn't take a slide rule or fancy chart to tell you when you're as cold as a well-digger's helper on the shady side of an iceberg.

# HOW TO COMPUTE CHILL FACTOR:

PROPERTY OF U.S. WEATHER BURRO

MARK WHEELER

YOU NEED TO KNOW TWO BASIC THINGS - WIND SPEED AND TEMPERATURE. TO DETERMINE WINDSPEED WITHOUT A GAUGE, RUN OR DRIVE IN THE SAME DIRECTION AS THE WIND IS BLOWING. TRY RUNNING FASTER OR SLOWER UNTIL YOU DON'T FEEL THE WIND BLOWING ANYMORE. HAVE A CAR (OR BOAT) WITH A SPEEDOMETER GO BESIDE YOU AND READ THE SPEEDOMETER.

OBTAIN THE TEMPERATURE WITH A THERMOMETER. ADD THE TWO NUMBERS TOGETHER, ADD YOUR AGE AND YOUR HAT SIZE. SUBTRACT YOUR ALASKA STATE INCOME TAX AND DIVIDE BY THE NUMBER OF SUBMARINE RIDES YOU'VE TAKEN SINCE 1952. MULTIPLY BY THE NUMBER OF STEPS IT IS OUT TO YOUR MAILBOX AND DIVIDE BY 326.795. TAKE OFF THE FIRST (OR LAST) TWO NUMBERS AND ROUND OFF THE NUMBER TO THE CLOSEST HUNDRED. THAT IS YOUR CHILL FACTOR (PLUS OR MINUS 75°).

45

## WEATHER

"United we stand, under the weather," was almost the official slogan for the 49th State. Everybody talks, lives, breathes, and plans for the weather. In Fairbanks it can get pretty cold for long periods and in Anchorage it's somewhat more mild. Then in Juneau it's even warmer and Ketchikan, warmer still. In summer it's much hotter in Fairbanks ($90°+$) than in Ket-

*The weather is not as bad as the climate.*

chikan, which cancels all the simple theories or other fibs you might hear about the weather.

WHEN THE WINTER TURNS TO FLURRIES, IT'S TIME TO PUT ON MORE FURRIES!

MARK WHEELER

46

# A VISITOR'S GUIDE TO THE WEATHER IN ALASKA...

## SPRING

APRIL SHOWERS BRING MAY FLOWERS... SO WILL A FLORIST...

"SORRY, BUT WHEN THE BIRDS ARE WALKING, I DON'T FLY!"

TO MAKE ALASKA DRY, DON'T DRINK!

THE ONLY WAY TO MAKE PARTS OF ALASKA DRY WOULD BE TO REDECLARE PROHIBITION...

## SUMMER

"THAT'S NO CLOUD...JUST A SWARM OF MOSQUITOES!"

HIGHEST OFFICIAL TEMP.- IN ALASKA (AND HAWAII) 100° - LOWEST: -78°

IN PRUDHOE BAY (WHERE ALL THE OIL IS) IT CAN BE -70° IN WINTER AND +90° IN SUMMER...

## AUTUMN

"GAD, IT'S RAINING HARD! IT IS REALLY COMIN' DOWN!"

"EVER SEEN IT RAINING UP?"

"YEA, I SAW IT RAINING UP IN FAIRBANKS!"

MOST ALASKANS TRAVEL THEMSELVES IN SEPTEMBER AND OCTOBER...

WHEN THE MUD GETS HARD, SNOW IS JUST AROUND THE CORNER...

OTHERWISE KNOWN AS FALL, AUTUMN IS...

## WINTER

WINTER IN ALASKA IS NOTHING TO SNEEZE AT...

"HELLO, WEATHER BUREAU? I JUST WANT YOU TO KNOW I JUST HAD TO PUT ON CHAINS TO GET THRU FOUR INCHES OF 'PARTLY CLOUDY'!"

HARD HAIL HURTS!

MARK WHEELER

47

# HOW TO FIND Mount McKinley

—POSSIBLE LOCATIONS OF MOUNT McKINLEY

① IF YOU LIVE ANYWHERE SOUTH OF 62° LATITUDE YOU'LL NEED TO TRAVEL NORTH, IF YOU LIVE AT 63° LATITUDE YOU CAN GO EITHER EAST OR WEST.

② LOOK FOR A VERY BIG MOUNTAIN

③ ON THE ALASKA RAILROAD - ASK THE CONDUCTOR.

④ IF YOU TAKE THE BUS, ASK THE DRIVER.

⑤ IF YOU GET LOST, ASK ANY MOOSE.

MARK WHEELER

## MOUNT McKINLEY

The highest mountain in North America is Mt. McKinley. The mountain was named that because when Alaska was purchased, the mountain was discovered to cover about $500 worth of land and President McKinley's picture is on a $500 bill. It had been called "Denali" by the natives but the historians found we have never had a president by that name.

DENALI:

DA BEAR DEN GONE AWAY!

PRONOUNCED LIKE "DEN-ALLEY". A "DEN" IS WHAT A BEAR LIVES IN AND AN "ALLEY" IS A KIND OF STREET BEHIND YOUR HOUSE. "DENALI" IS WHAT YOU CALL THE DOMICILE OF YOUR BACK YARD BEAR OR "HIS ROOM" INSIDE YOUR HOUSE.

*Mount McKinley is not only the highest mountain in North America but is also the highest in Alaska.*

48

MARK WHEELER

"I thought all Alaskans would be expert skiers. . ."

49

*"Now gentlemen, with this poster and brochure, thousands, maybe millions, of tourists will add Kotzebue to their travel plans . . . can you just imagine it. . .?"*

50

## KOTZEBUE

Kotzebue is about 50 miles north of the Arctic Circle and somewhat above it. For years and years it was a native village, and today can't find any excuse to change. One of the more exciting things to do there is to watch water alternately freeze and melt, which it does every year.

In the summer (last year on a Thursday afternoon) the eskimos have a native festival which includes a game to see how far one can toss a blanket. Also the eskimos dance (known as "cutting up the floor") and carve (known as "cutting up the ivory or jade") and will show you how to paddle (or spank) a kayak which is a boat for one person, so don't be offended if you are told to, "go paddle your own canoe to Kotzebue."

*The Arctic Circle is a navigational hazard.*

IF YOU'RE FEELING BLUE, VISIT KOTZEBUE! BECAUSE THERE IS SO MUCH TO SEE & DO:

YOU CAN GO FIND A WHALE...OR ENJOY THE MIDNIGHT SUN FOR 36 DAYS STRAIGHT...OR SEE THE ESKIMO DANCERS...OR BUY THE NATIVE ARTS & CRAFTS ...OR HAVE A RIDE IN AN OOMIAK...OR GET SOME JADE...OR

ESKIMO: A PERSON WHO IS NATIVE TO THE ARCTIC REGIONS OF ALASKA, CANADA, GREENLAND, & SIBERIA. *USUALLY WEARS A PARKA. VERY HARD TO TELL WHICH IS WHICH IS WHICH OF SEXES. *SOME ESKIMOS WEAR "ESKIMONOS."

51

"... and how much money will you need to build this igloo?"

52

"I tell you George, they have a 21 cubic foot freezer in there . . . I saw it myself!"

MARK WHEELER

53

"I WARNED HER NOT TO DIVE TOO MUCH SO CLOSE TO FREEZE UP!"

MARK WHEELER

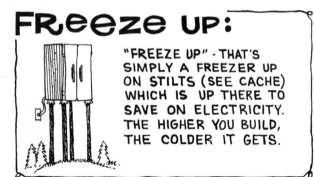

# FReeze up:

"FREEZE UP" - THAT'S SIMPLY A FREEZER UP ON STILTS (SEE CACHE) WHICH IS UP THERE TO SAVE ON ELECTRICITY. THE HIGHER YOU BUILD, THE COLDER IT GETS.

*Alaska is between Alabama and Arizona . . . (alphabetically).*

## FREEZE-UP

At 32° water freezes. The longer it is 32 or below, the more water will freeze. At 50° below you can guess what else will freeze . . . pronto.

At freeze-up most everything stops, except you going downhill in your car. With everything slowing down, a condition known as permafrost happens. At freeze-up, permafrost (scientifically explained elsewhere) becomes even more perma.

The problem with the stuff is that it does melt a little in the summer. It melts just enough to make things pretty muddy and, if you build a house on it, you might find it canted over to one side just a bit because the ground never melts evenly.

Real Estate agents always have a tough time, and when faced with having to sell these houses that now are leaning over every which way, they got a brilliant idea. Real Estate people refer to these houses as being "Listed."

54

MARK WHEELER

"Of course next winter all you have to do is keep a fire in the fireplace and shovel the driveway, and some neighbor kid can do that. . ."

55

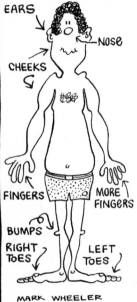

## HOW TO KNOW WHEN YOU HAVE
# FROSTBITE

EARS → NOSE

CHEEKS

FINGERS  MORE FINGERS

BUMPS

RIGHT TOES  LEFT TOES

MARK WHEELER

IF YOU'RE OUT IN SUPER-COLD WEATHER AND YOUR FEET HURT, YOU'RE OK.
IF YOUR FEET (OR HANDS, OR EARS, OR ETC.) DO NOT HURT, YOU CAN BET THEY ARE FROST BITTEN.

FROSTBITE FIRST SHOWS AS A WHITE PATCH ON THE SKIN. THE REMEDY IS TO SOAK THE AREA IN 107° WATER (NOT HOTTER) UNTIL THE COLOR RETURNS. IF THE COLOR DOES NOT RETURN, YOU ARE PROBABLY DEAD SO DON'T WORRY ABOUT IT. WARNING: FROSTBITE AIN'T VERY MUCH FUN!

56

# FROST BITE:

"FROST BITE" IS WHAT YOU HAVE IF YOU ARE BITTEN BY A FUNNY MAN NAMED JACK FROST WHO WILL NIBBLE ON YOUR EXTREMITIES (NOSE, EARS, FINGERS, TOES, ETC.) IF YOU'RE NOT CAREFUL IN COLD WEATHER.

COLOR HIM BLUE!

*Frostbite is rare in Hawaii.*

## FROST BITE

Frost Bite is nothing like a mosquito bite or a fish bite. Frost Bite is caused by actual freezing of the skin usually due to a lack of circulation. It attacks fingers and toes first and in some ethnic groups it affects the brain areas too. The best remedy is to soak the affected area in 107° water even if the affected area is your head.

"You heard me . . . frostbit or not . . . both of you scram!"

MARK WHEELER

SEARS & ROEBUCK 1898

57

"... and the seagulls in Alaska all have this holier-than-thou attitude!"

58

A VISITOR'S GUIDE TO THE SEALS OF ALASKA:

RIBBON SEAL:

FUR SEAL: (SAME AS 'SEAL OF APPROVAL')

EASTER SEAL:

HAIR SEAL:

CHRISTMAS SEAL:

STATE SEAL: ★ALASKA

MARK WHEELER

*Most Alaskan seals are never licked.*

FUR SEAL: "FUR" IS THE FUZZY OUTER LAYER OF AN ANIMAL AND A "SEAL" IS LIKE THE ALASKA STATE SEAL OR AN ENVELOPE SEAL. A FUR SEAL CAN BE EITHER A FUZZY COAT OF ARMS OR A FUZZY ENVELOPE (ILLUSTRATED).

## SEALS

Most seals travel in "Herds." A herd is somewhat like a Ford only bigger (like a double station wagon). You might already know about herds from cows or sheep but if not, please don't worry about it. Just remember that what looks like a bunch of seals is really a herd, but, after all, what do you care what the seals heard?

59

"If that Polar Bear starts after us, I'll take the dogs and you climb the tallest tree you can find!"

MARK WHEELER

60

# BARROW

An English geographer and promoter, John Barrow (and his brother, Wheel) went discovering one day and bumped into a point of land that wasn't on the chart. In looking for a name for the point he discovered that he hadn't named anything after himself yet. Quick to remedy the situation he named Point Barrow, which now includes Barrow which is the most northern town in North (naturally) America.

One of the most interesting things about Barrow is the weather. In Barrow the sun is alternately shy and bold. Winter beats the daylights out of it, whereas in the summer it stays up about 80 days straight during May, June, and July. That's what is known as the Midnight Sun which is one reason why Drive-In Movies aren't so popular up there.

*The year around average temperature in Barrow is only 10° above zero.*

JOHN BARROW
·EXPLORER·

MARK WHEELER

61

"Back in '98 I was just a kid . . . went over the pass and struck it real big . . . just got back to town yesterday . . . guess I was luckier than some. . ."

62

## GOLD FEVER (Klondikeitus)

Gold Fever has many strange symptoms and even stranger cures. Among the symptoms are glazed eyes, groping hands, and an unsteady walk. Some sufferers also mumble phrases like, "There's gold in them thar hills!", and such.

The sad parts of the gold fever problem are (a) lack of gold, (b) lack of lust for it, and (c) lack of a market for it once you get it. So few couples are getting married these days that gold for wedding rings is just not in demand and dentists are using less due to advances in synthetic filling materials.

Today, gold fever has changed from a lust for yellow gold to a lust for black gold, and white gold is being discussed. This kind of polarization isn't helping the epidemic much but it is perpetuating the drilling business but not the kind dentists do. . .

*Klondikeitus can not be cured with aspirin or whiskey.*

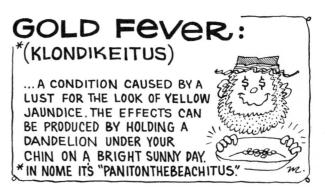

63

MARK WHEELER

"All this rain makes more water in the water which makes more space between fish. . ."

64

**WHAT TO DO IF A MOOSE GIVES YOU A FUNNY LOOK:**

THE MOOSE WILL... LOOK AT YOU CROSSEYED AND MAY STICK OUT HIS TONGUE AT YOU. HE MAY ALSO PAW THE GROUND, SHIFT HIS WEIGHT, SNORT, AND CONTINUE TO STARE AT YOU FOR LONG PERIODS WITHOUT BLINKING. TAKE EXTREME CARE ...

AND YOU SHOULD... TRY TO FIND OUT WHAT HE WANTS...OR IF HE IS JUST LONELY...OR IF HE IS HUNGRY. THE BEST THING TO DO IS TO KEEP HIM TALKING...ABOUT ANYTHING...HIS WIFE, FAMILY, KIDS, ETC. OR TRY TO ENTERTAIN HIM WITH A SONG OR DANCE OR BY MAKING FUNNY FACES OR BY STICKING YOUR FINGERS IN YOUR EARS AND GOING,"BLAH."

## FISHING IN THE RAIN

In one place in Alaska it rains 18 feet of water (naturally) per year. Rubber duck sales here are the highest in the State. The rain causes several problems though. With so much rain the worms used for fishing are mistaken for fish themselves. They grow fins, spawn upstream, and go to the fishes' schools, and win first prize in the fishes' masquerade parties every time. Fish rarely eat other fishy looking fish.

*Sticking your tongue out at him won't affect the charge of a bull moose.*

## WEATHER

Alaska is truly a land of contrast. Jack Frost went on strike a few years ago. He wanted more days off. Specifically he wanted the 4th of July and Mother's Day. At Fort Yukon, Alaska, the temperature went from about 70° below zero to 100° above in the same year.

The statistics don't say exactly what time of the year these phenomena took place but I would bet my mukluks the 100° above didn't happen in January.

67

*"Ticket please."*

66

## GOOSE FLYING

It is fairly easy to tell the amphibious airplane known as a "goose" from the bird by the same name. The bird furiously flaps its wings while the plane just flaps its flaps. Both are usually found in one of three places, either flying in the air (where else?) or sitting on the water, or on the land.

The airplanes carry passengers and have two propellers. The birds do not usually carry passengers and have no visible means of propulsion.

In Alaska more people would rather fly in an amphibious craft because of the immediate availability of places to land without requiring the facilities of a formal tax-supported airport should an emergency arise.

To someone who has never flown in a goose before it can give you quite a start, especially if you take off from land but don't land on land.

67

"We'll have two grub steaks . . . medium rare. . ."

68

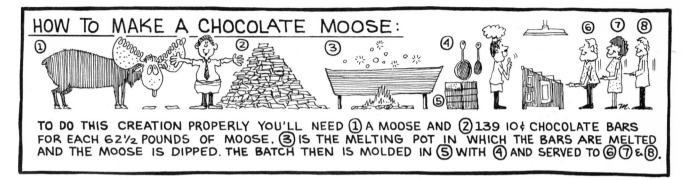

**HOW TO MAKE A CHOCOLATE MOOSE:**

TO DO THIS CREATION PROPERLY YOU'LL NEED ① A MOOSE AND ② 139 10¢ CHOCOLATE BARS FOR EACH 62½ POUNDS OF MOOSE. ③ IS THE MELTING POT IN WHICH THE BARS ARE MELTED AND THE MOOSE IS DIPPED. THE BATCH THEN IS MOLDED IN ⑤ WITH ④ AND SERVED TO ⑥ ⑦ & ⑧.

*Alaska ranks 50th in pineapple production in the country.*

**GRUBSTAKE:**

"GRUBSTAKE," THAT'S A TOMBSTONE FOR A DEAD GRUB.
(ESPECIALLY ALASKAN GRUBS)

RIP

**OR GRUBSTEAK:**
BEST ORDERED MEDIUM-RARE WITH A BAKED POTATO.

MOOSEMEAT IS BEST...

## GRUBSTAKE/GRUBSTEAK

To end the confusion over the difference between a "grubstake" and a "grubsteak," be now introduced to the dissimilarities. One is tough and the other is tougher. One is packed carefully while the other is also. One is cherished and revered as a delicacy, and, here the separation is apparent, the other is coddled and protected. A Grubsteak can be medium rare but, many times, a good Grubstake is extremely rare.

69

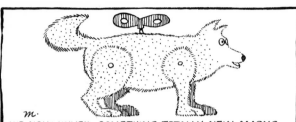

WE NOW UNVEIL SOMETHING TOTALLY NEW AMONG DOGS. THIS RIG IS A WIND-UP VERSION OF THE POPULAR SLED PULLER. IT WILL GO A MILE PER WIND AND DOESN'T EAT MUCH. VERY CLEVER!

# HUSKY: CAN BE...
1. THE OFFICIAL MASCOT OF THE UNIVERSITY OF WASHINGTON. (NOT IN ALASKA)
2. THE QUALITY OF BEING THAT WAY.
3. AN ALASKAN DOG KNOWN FOR HIS ABILITY TO TRAVEL GREAT DISTANCES AND LIVE ON MUSH.
4. ALL OF THE ABOVE.
5. NONE OF THE ABOVE.

## HUSKY

A whole bunch of Alaskans classify themselves as "Husky." Actually the term was not created in Alaska but in far off Iowa. This well known midwest state is known as the corn capital of the U.S.A. In order to be eaten with some finesse, the corn must first be husked. A person who husks corn is known as a "husker." Through the ages the term was transposed into "husky" through a myriad of dialects.

Later the word became a term of endearment for various dogs. What dogs ever had to do with corn is not clear except for the popular snack combining a hot dog wrapped in a corn fritter available at carnivals.

Husky is an overall term. These overalls are primarily worn by dogs that pull sleds. Dogs that pull sleds are also called Huskies (which is plural for Husky). Most huskies wear Husky overalls but (since they can't talk) won't admit it. Most huskies are shy about this and would probably think you stupid for asking about it.

70

"Naturally he isn't much on looks but you should see him pull a sled. . ."

MARK WHEELER

71

"We were going to Hawaii this winter but ran short on cash so we're going to next best . . . Anchorage!"

MARK WHEELER

72

## FAIRBANKS

Fairbanks used to be two words. Legend has it that a bank examiner came along checking and scribbling things on a form on his clipboard. He checked the National, First, Alaska State, and a bunch of others "Excellent," then he checked the banks of the Yukon, and gave them a "Good," and last he checked the banks of the Chena and rated them "Fair."

The old sourdough sitting on and admiring the banks of the Chena said, "You really can't ask for anything more than fair banks," and the name stuck.

Today Fairbanks is alternately hot, cold & colder. It can be close to 100° above in the summer and not far from 60° below all the other times. Fall and Spring were cancelled years ago due to a lack of interest.

*Fairbanks was actually named for Charles W. Fairbanks, Vice President for Teddy Roosevelt.*

**HANDY THINGS TO HAVE OR BE, IN THE WINTER, IN FAIRBANKS:**

...ALL VERY HANDY...

1. HAVE A HEATED CONVERSATION.
2. BE HOT UNDER THE COLLAR.
3. HAVE A WARM PERSONALITY.
4. HAVE A SUNNY OUTLOOK.
5. HAVE A HOT FOOT.
6. A DOUBLE BED WARMER.
7. HAVE A DOUBLE BED.
8. A POT-BELLIED STOVE.
9. COLD CASH.

**ICE FOG:** EMBARRASSING

A KIND OF GOOPY OILY FOG WHICH HAPPENS WHEN IT'S SUPER COLD AND THERE IS NO WIND TO MOVE THE AIR POLLUTION...UGH!!!

73

## ICEBERGS

At 32° water freezes. That is, it turns from a liquid to a solid. This solid has been known to have had ships bump into it, have polar bears live on it, have ice worms live in it, and Eskimos try not to fall off of it. Ice does serve useful purposes though, as anyone who has frequented a bar knows. Most icebergs are former glaciers.

## ICEBERG:

SOMETIMES SPELLED "ICEBURG" (WHICH IS NOTHING LIKE PITTSBURG). THE WORD IS USED WHEN COMPARING TOWNS LIKE BARROW, NOME, UNALAKLEET, AND FORT YUKON IN THE WINTER TIME TO EXPRESS HOW COLD THEY ARE, OR THAT 9/10 ths OF THE PLACE HAPPENS TO BE UNDERWATER.

HERE NOW IS YOUR VERY OWN
(TAKE IT OR LEAVE IT)
ALASKA HIGHWAY CHECK LIST

| T L DK | ITEM | T L DK | ITEM |
|---|---|---|---|
| ☐☐☐ | FISHING POLE | ☐☐☐ | CHRISTMAS LIST |
| ☐☐☐ | WIFE | ☐☐☐ | SUN-TAN LOTION |
| ☐☐☐ | KID #1 | ☐☐☐ | TRAVELLERS CHECKS |
| ☐☐☐ | KID #2 | ☐☐☐ | EXTRA MAP OF UTAH |
| ☐☐☐ | KID #3 | ☐☐☐ | HALLOWEEN MASK |
| ☐☐☐ | ADDITIONAL KIDS | ☐☐☐ | CAR |
| ☐☐☐ | WATERSKIS | ☐☐☐ | BATTERY FOR WATCH |
| ☐☐☐ | SURVIVAL KIT FOR SELF | ☐☐☐ | DOG FOOD |
| ☐☐☐ | SURVIVAL KIT FOR WIFE | ☐☐☐ | CAMERA |
| ☐☐☐ | SURVIVAL KITS FOR KIDS | ☐☐☐ | RUBBER DUCK |
| | | ☐☐☐ | ANTI-MOSQUITO STUFF |
| ☐☐☐ | GOLF CLUBS | ☐☐☐ | SUNGLASSES |
| ☐☐☐ | TUXEDO | ☐☐☐ | EXERCISE MACHINE |
| ☐☐☐ | PET SNAKE | ☐☐☐ | SLINGSHOT |
| ☐☐☐ | SECRETARY | ☐☐☐ | TAXIDERMY KIT |
| ☐☐☐ | EXTRA SOCKS | ☐☐☐ | FILM |
| ☐☐☐ | GIEGER COUNTER | ☐☐☐ | A GOOD BOOK |
| ☐☐☐ | MOOSE CALL | ☐☐☐ | RIVER RAFT |
| ☐☐☐ | PORTABLE T.V. | ☐☐☐ | MONEY CONVERTER |
| | | ☐ | MOTHER-IN-LAW |

T · TAKE IT    L · LEAVE IT    DK · DON'T KNOW

*The Alcan Highway took 10,000 men to build. Mosquitoes kidnapped 34 of them.*

74

HAZARDS TO BE MINDFUL OF ON THE ALASKA HIGHWAY:

EYE STRAIN FROM LOOKING AT ALL THE SCENERY

OVER ZEALOUS ANIMALS

STILL MORE DUST

←DUST
MORE DUST

PUT TAPE ON ALL THINGS YOU DON'T WANT FULL OF DUST

PROTECT HEAD-LIGHTS FROM ROCKS!

CUSHION → YOUR GAS TANK AGAINST PUNCTURES BY SHARP ROCKS

FLYING ROCKS →

THE HIGHWAY IS DUSTIER ON THE CANADIAN SIDE. BE CAREFUL WITH FIRE!

TAKE LOTS OF BUG REPELLANTS!

TAPE THE SEAMS ON YOUR LUGGAGE TO KEEP OUT DUST!

MAKE SURE YOUR CAR IS IN PERFECT MECHANICAL CONDITION BEFORE YOU START!

MARK WHEELER

OTHER HANDY STUFF YOU SHOULD KEEP UPPERMOST IN YOUR MIND FROM TIME TO TIME 'CAUSE YA MIGHT NEED IT:

• PACK AN EXTRA FAN BELT, POINTS, CONDENSER, SPARK PLUGS, TIRE CHAINS (GOOD IN MUD TOO) A CAN OR TWO OF OIL, TWO SPARE TIRES, HEADLIGHT, PLUS WHATEVER ELSE YOU THINK YOU MIGHT NEED.

• REMEMBER BUGS WILL GET IN YOUR RADIATOR AND WILL CAUSE YOUR ENGINE TO OVERHEAT.

• THERE IS A $500 FINE FOR LITTERING...ENFORCED!

• BE CAREFUL WITH FIRE!

• BE CAREFUL WITH YOURSELF!

*Roads are as scarce as hens themselves in southeastern Alaska.*

75

*Gold was discovered in the Klondike August 16, 1896 near Whitehorse.*

HEADQUARTERS
YUKON TERRITORY
ROYAL CANADIAN
MOUNTED
POLICE
WHITEHORSE, Y.T.

MARK WHEELER

*"Excuse me Sergeant . . . Do you know where we can find SGT. PRESTON of the Yukon and his faithful dog, KING?"*

76

## WHITEHORSE

Whitehorse is not in Alaska but played a very important part in the history of Alaska, especially in the days of the Gold Rush. What is more romantic is that Whitehorse is the capital of the Yukon Territory. Also it is the northern terminus for one of the greatest trips around, the White Pass and Yukon Railroad trip to Skagway.

## IGLOOS

Most tourists think everyone in Alaska lives in igloos. Nothing could be further from the truth. You may have heard that in many places it even gets above freezing in parts of Alaska. Naturally snow is frozen water and it takes snow (with ice) to build an igloo. To believe your house might melt at any given moment is hard on your nerves, and even harder on the assessor. . . .

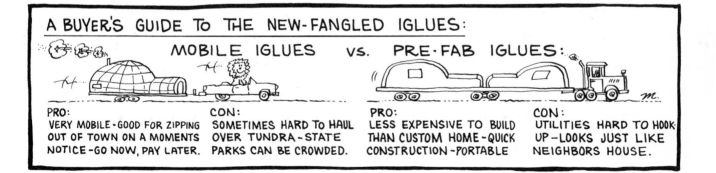

A BUYER'S GUIDE TO THE NEW-FANGLED IGLUES:

MOBILE IGLUES vs. PRE-FAB IGLUES:

PRO:
VERY MOBILE-GOOD FOR ZIPPING OUT OF TOWN ON A MOMENTS NOTICE-GO NOW, PAY LATER.

CON:
SOMETIMES HARD TO HAUL OVER TUNDRA-STATE PARKS CAN BE CROWDED.

PRO:
LESS EXPENSIVE TO BUILD THAN CUSTOM HOME-QUICK CONSTRUCTION -PORTABLE

CON:
UTILITIES HARD TO HOOK UP-LOOKS JUST LIKE NEIGHBORS HOUSE.

77

*"Oogruk is planning on building a basement too. . ."*

MARK WHEELER

## HOW TO BUILD AN IGLOO:

First you head for your local newstand to pick up the latest copies of "Good Iglookeeping," "Igloos and Gardens," and "Igloos Beautiful." Flip through them and take particular note of entryways, attics, basements, patios, decks, porches, and/or family or recreation rooms. Tear out all the good ideas and assemble them into a planning book. Take your book to an architect and discuss the size and terrain of your land. Also discuss your budget and your building schedule.

When you firmly have a set of detailed plans go to the bank. Discuss F.H.A., V.A., or Conventional Loans and sign your life away.

Be sure to get a reputable building contractor. Supervise all steps of construction including double checking faucets and electrical outlets.

Move in upon completion and have a housewarming party but when doing so, a note of caution is advised.

An Eskimo can do all this in 40 minutes.

MARK WHEELER

IGLOO: (IGLEW, IGLUE, IGLOU, OR IGLU)

ONE EA. IG.

STICKY STUFF USED TO GLUE IGS TOGETHER. IF YOU COLLECT AND GLUE ENOUGH IGS AND PUT WHEELS UNDER IT, YOU'LL HAVE AN "IGMOBILE".

79

## HOW TO MAKE SENSE OUT OF A
## TIDE CHART

1. MAKE SURE YOU HAVE:
   - THE RIGHT CHART?
   - THE CURRENT YEAR?
   - THE CORRECT TIME?
   - THE RIGHT PLACE?
   - THE WIND DIRECTION?

2. SEE IF YOU ARE ON SOMETHING WHICH WILL FLOAT.
3. CONSULT A FISH WHO HAS BEEN AROUND
4. HOLD CHART RIGHT-SIDE-UP.

WHAT TO DO WHEN THE
*TIDE GOES OUT

1. WAIT
2. WAIT SOME MORE
3. CONTINUE TO WAIT UNTIL IT COMES BACK IN AGAIN...

ALL TIDES ARE AFFECTED BY MOONSHINE...

MARK WHEELER

*ALASKA HAS SOME OF THE HIGHEST & LOWEST TIDES IN THE WORLD!

Herring fishing supplies are known as herring aids.

80

# KING CRAB:

A "KING" IS A KIND OF SOVEREIGN RULER (LIKE A YARD STICK) AND A "CRAB" IS LIKE AN OLD CRAB, SO A KING CRAB MUST EITHER BE AN OLD 3 FOOT CRAB OR AN OLD GRUMPY YARDSTICK."

**KING CRAB**

King Crab is a type of crab which is making Alaska better known. As far as the word "King" goes, it is used in lots of terms in Alaska like, "King Salmon" and, "King Island." One should expect Scallops, Halibut, Clams, and Shrimp will follow in all their regal splendor. King Salmon are easily identified by the crowns on their heads and the surfs they have around them.

*"Gotta Tide Chart?"*

MARK WHEELER

Sign in cartoon: SALMON DERBY STARTS FRIDAY

81

"One of these days when my net is so full I can walk across it, I'm going to think about nothin' except that lousy $7,862.86 I owe you."

82

## BOAT YARDS

Boat yards in Alaska are something over three feet. Here boats are built, repaired, serviced, and seldom paid for. A good mechanic specializing in boats has an appointment book much like a dentist or hairdresser.

Most boat yards have a lot of winches hanging around. These winches might include the mechanics wife and/or mother-in-law. Also boat yards are usually built on or near the water primarily because that's where the boats are.

When a fisherman has a good season the boat yard gets paid. When the fisherman has a bad season, the boat yard owner starts looking for a cemetery in need of a new sign. It turns out to be a pretty good deal for the cemetery because all they have to do is change the letters "AT" in "BOAT" to "NE," and the cemetery can have a new sign.

Most boat yard owners don't go that far though. They just caulk the "no-pay" boats with water soluble glue. . .

## TYPES OF BOATS

You might like to know which type of boat is which in Alaskan waters. Here is a pick-and-choose list: Gravy Boats, Trollers, Seiners, Halibut Boats, Crab Boats, White Boats, Long Boats, Short Boats, Good Boats, Row Boats, Slow Boats, Volga Boats, Sail Boats, Ice Boats, Leaky Boats, Rotted Boats, Fiberglass Boats, Twin-Screwed Boats, and Paddle Boats. All the rest are ships.

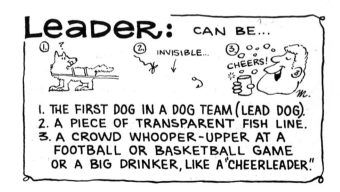

Leader: CAN BE...
1. THE FIRST DOG IN A DOG TEAM (LEAD DOG).
2. A PIECE OF TRANSPARENT FISH LINE.
3. A CROWD WHOOPER-UPPER AT A FOOTBALL OR BASKETBALL GAME OR A BIG DRINKER, LIKE A "CHEERLEADER."

WHERE THE SUN DOESN'T GO IN THE LAND OF THE MIDNIGHT SUN:

⌐ CAUTION: HORIZON - DO NOT GO BELOW THIS LINE FOR AT LEAST 60 DAYS DURIN' SUMMER...

## MIDNIGHT SUN

The midnight sun is just that. It stays light all night, which is one reason why drive-in movies aren't so popular. In the winter it stays dark maybe 21 hours a day but at 50° below your popcorn freezes. Being light all night also has something to do with the lack of population growth too, but the scientists say this problem requires further study.

**MIDNIGHT SUN:**
(ACTUAL TIME LAPSE PHOTO OF SUN: TIME: 3 MINUTES)

ACTUALLY THE MIDNIGHT SUN IS THE SAME SUN AS ANY OTHER SUN EXCEPT THIS SUN CAN BE SEEN AT TIMES WHEN PEOPLE IN OTHER PLACES IN THE WORLD CAN'T SEE IT BECAUSE IT IS NIGHTTIME, BUT, ALTHOUGH THE CLOCK SAYS

84

MARK WHEELER

*"Let's fly over to Kodiak and see what the fishermen are using for bait today. . ."*

85

*"Martha . . . please . . . I've had enough crabbing for now!"*

MARK WHEELER

86

## KODIAK

Kodiak (the town) is on Kodiak (the island). Kodiak is sometimes called the Garden Isle because (except for the lack of palm trees) it looks so much like Kauai in Hawaii.

Kodiak is famous for its photogenic bears called Kodak Bears. These are the bears Navy commanders caution their men against wrestling with the suggestion, "When you get to town, kiss yourself a pretty girl and wrestle yourself a bear but make sure you don't get 'em mixed up!"

The famous King Crab comes from here. Only male crabs are kept for canning which is why the females have such a membership in their Lonely Hearts Club. If you are a male crab who fancies a well turned leg, Kodiak is sure to quicken your pulse.

In 1791 Kodiak had to be rebuilt by the Russlans after the Kodiak they built in 1784 accidentally went out with the tide one day.

Nowadays fishing and crabbing (mostly about the fishing) keep Kodiakites occupied when they're not chasing the Russian or Japanese fishing fleets.

87

## BROWNIE QUIZ

To alleviate some of the confusion about the bears which are sometimes called "Brownies" one must learn the difference between all three kinds of brownies; Bears, Cookies, and Junior Girl Scouts. To sort them out, complete the following quiz using the symbols "BB" (Brown Bears) "BC" (Brownie Cookies) and "JGS" (Junior Girl Scouts).

1. Which brownies eat people?
2. Which brownies do people eat?
3. Which brownies are eaten by other brownies?
4. Which brownies are hunted?
5. Which brownies have four legs?
6. Which brownies do not have two eyes?
7. Which brownies are baked in the oven?
8. Which brownies meet on Tuesdays?
9. Which brownies are all girls?
10. Which brownies are partly girls?
11. Which brownies taste best with milk?
12. Which brownies hibernate in the winter?
13. Which brownies do not eat huckleberries?
14. Which brownies earn merit badges?
15. Which brownies do not eat fish?

## WHICH KIND OF BROWNIE WOULD YOU LIKE TO HAVE IN YOUR OVEN?

## MUKLUKS

Mukluks are somewhat like boots which most people wear on their feet. They are made from fur with some fur inside and some fur outside. You wear one on each foot which is probably why they come in pairs. If one desires mukluk hip boots one must get his own rubber hip boots to which he can paste on his own fur. Mukluks are required when traveling in the Arctic, which is why the eskimos invented them.

*You can run amuck in your mukluks.*

MUKLUK: "...and have good mukluk!"

"MUKLUK", IS A COMBINATION OF "MUCK" WHICH IS MUD, AND "LUCK" WHICH IS GOOD (OR ILL) FORTUNE. "MUCK LUCK" OR "MUKLUK" IS LIKE SAYING "GOOD LUCK" IN THE RAINY SEASON.

88

*"With only two trains in Alaska, box cars are hard to find, and from Skagway south a log raft will get you any-where you want to go. . ."*

MARK WHEELER

89

...AND DON'T FORGET SPENARD!

ANCHORAGE HAS A REAL SUBURB JUST LIKE THE ONE YOU LIVE IN OR HAVE RIGHT NEAR YOUR TOWN. SPENARD IS VERY COZY WITH ANCHORAGE AND ANCHORAGE (AS WELL AS THE REST OF THE STATE) IS SO COZY WITH SEATTLE THAT ALL TOGETHER THEY FORM ONE STATISTICAL MARKETING AREA...
HOW DISGUSTING!

MUSHER:

"MUSH" IS THE POPULAR BREAKFAST DISH BUT IN ALASKA IT IS MADE FROM MUSH-ROOMS AND A "MUSHER" IS ONE WHO EATS THIS SPECIAL PORRIDGE.

90

## ANCHORAGE

Anchorage is the largest city in Alaska. It is advertised as the Air Crossroads of the world. On the globe you'll easily find Anchorage half way between Samoa and Algiers (or vice versa) and therefore is a good place to land and get gassed.

Anchorage is also about half way between Taiwan and the Panama Canal but not too many go that way around.

You can get a pretty good idea what Alaska has to offer the traveler by shopping in the gift shop at the Anchorage Airport unless you bought this book there. Their gift selection is about the biggest in the State.

You might be interested to know there is a place called Anchorage, Kentucky. Anchorage, Alaska has an elevation of 118 feet which makes it three feet higher than Holyoke, Massachusetts, a fact in which you might not be interested.

*The longitude of Anchorage varies occasionally.*

CHORAGE FUR RENDEZVOUS
SLED DOG CHAMPIONSHIPS

START

MARK WHEELER

"I believe the word is 'MUSH', not, 'Ya'll get along there little doggies'!"

**WHAT IS GOOD ABOUT MUSKEG:**

IN THE WORDS OF THE OLD SOURDOUGH PHILOSOPHER, MR. AL A. SKA, (NABBER OF COUNTLESS BEARS, GOATS, AND MOOSES; VICTIM OF THREE MOSQUITO BITES, ALL FATAL; WINNER OF THE ICE WORM LOOK ALIKE CONTEST; AND FULL TIME DIRTY OLD MAN), "MUSKEG IS NO *@"xZ@꜀X GOOD!"

MARK WHEELER

**MUSK KEG:**

"MUSK" IS FROM "MUSK OX" (THE ANIMAL WITH FUNNY HORNS) AND A "KEG" IS A TYPE OF BARREL. PUT THEM TOGETHER AND YOU LEARN THAT "MUSK KEG" (OR "MUSKEG") IS A BARREL WITH FUNNY HORNS THAT'S HARD TO WALK ON.

(FOUND ALL OVER ALASKA)

## MUSKEG

Muskeg is otherwise known as a style of soggy buggy bog or a mushy gooshy mossy mess. When you walk on it you'll hear a squishy sound and you'll hear the same sound back on hard ground if your boots aren't waterproof.

Muskeg grows best around slow drainage areas and many mosquitoes know how to make a house out of it very much like a robin builds a nest out of twigs and string.

There is an abundance of muskeg around in the upper plains in the mountains and many a hiker has sworn at it rather than by it.

**MUSKEG** SHOULD NOT BE WORN IN THE SOCKS OR HIP BOOTS...

92

## HOW TO TELL THE DIFFERENCE BETWEEN a MUSK OX AND a POLAR BEAR:

**A MUSK OX HAS:** FOUR HOOFS... FUNNY HORNS... TWO EYES... A NOSE... SOFT KNITTABLE WOOL CALLED "QIVIUT" (RHYMES WITH "DIVOT")... FUNNY RELATIVES... A SIMPLE DIET... NO DESIRE TO HUNT SEALS ...A BASIC FEAR OF WOLVES... SAFETY IN NUMBERS... ENDURANCE... HEAVY COAT... MANY FRIENDS (BUT NOT ENOUGH).

**A POLAR BEAR HAS:** MORE LETTERS IN IT'S NAME... FOUR PAWS (NOT TO BE CONFUSED WITH PAS, LIKE FATHERS)... MORE WHITE FUR... NO HORNS... LESS GRASS TO EAT... CAN'T CLIMB TREES... BASIC FEAR OF NOTHING... ENDURANCE... HEAVY COAT... QUITE A FEW FRIENDS (BUT NOT ENOUGH).

MARK WHEELER

# MUSK OX:

"MUSK", IS FROM THE WORD "MUSKET" WHICH IS AN OLD TYPE OF GUN, AND "OX", WHICH IS FROM THE WORD "OXYGEN" WHICH IS A PART OF AIR, ALL COMBINE INTO "MUSK OX" WHICH IS A TYPE OF AIR GUN. (PROBABLY SHOOTS A BUNCH OF HOT AIR)

CAN BLOW A MOOSE DOWN FROM A GOOD 20" AWAY...

MUST BE CUSTOM BUILT

## MUSK OX

Some musk ox prefer to be called "oxen" but that term seems to better befit a beast of burden which the musk ox isn't. Musk ox, although once almost extinct, are now being raised for their "Qiviut" which is a fuzzy fine wool. One nice thing about the wool is that the animal can run around growing more which they seem to do with very little help.

93

"I need a salmon and a couple pounds of shrimp right away."

MARK WHEELER

94

## PETERSBURG

Peter and Getty Svendsen discovered Petersburg and Gettysburg (respectively) and later their son William discovered Hoboken, New Jersey.

Petersburg has been called lots of things but prefers to be known as "Little Norway of Alaska." The title was first awarded to Petersburg because nobody else applied for it and the telephone book has only three different surnames (all Norwegian), fifty-one Christian names (mostly Norwegian), and every middle initial you can think of (all confusing).

Most of the people in Petersburg are actually from a country called "The Old" and some don't even speak Alaskan.

Fishing and shrimping are the main things Petersburgers (like in ham) do. The homes are mainly gingerbread (the exceptions are wood or cement or mobile) and there is a Scandinavian flavor to the architecture. A visit to Petersburg surely will remind you of home especially if you were born in Oslo.

*Petersburg had the first traffic light in Alaska (1938).*

**NaTive:** IN ALASKA THIS WORD IS FROM "NATIVITY" (THE FESTIVAL OF ONE'S BIRTH) IN ONE SPECIFIC PLACE (ORIGINALLY) RATHER THAN SOME ONE WHO WAS BORN IN TWO (OR MORE) PLACES LIKE MANY NEW "NATIVES."

## NATIVE

Natives are usually people (though not a specific requirement) who, with their mothers, were in Alaska when the blessed event of their nativity happened. Naturally this event should only happen in one place, but many Alaskans have foregone the above and labeled themselves natives although, in truth, very few are. All Alaskans however toot about being native regardless, especially when the Native Land Claims Bill is being discussed.

95

MARK WHEELER

*". . . and just beyond wells number 42, 43, and 44 will be the refinery, and. . ."*

96

# NORTH SLOPE OIL

About 20 percent of the land area in the U.S. is being poked around on just to find the stuff that leaks out of our car engines onto the highway. Some of that area is on what's called the North Slope of the Brooks Mountain Range in Alaska more commonly known simply as "The North Slope."

Oil is the name and money is the game. So is ecology, environmental sciences, and a whole rigfull of problems.

Of course oil is very important to all of us. Without it we couldn't cook deep fried chicken, we would all get sun burned, we would have nothing to go with vinegar on our salads and our airplanes, trains, cars, trucks, and buses would have to run on electricity.

So would our furnaces, stoves, lawnmowers, outboard boat motors, and hand warmers. In other words if it wasn't for oil we would need so much electricity that there wouldn't be any room left in the sky for any more kites . . . with or without keys.

OIL COMES IN:
GUSHERS:
DRUMS:
CANS:
TANKERS (TANKARDS):

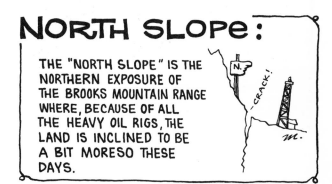

NORTH SLOPE:

THE "NORTH SLOPE" IS THE NORTHERN EXPOSURE OF THE BROOKS MOUNTAIN RANGE WHERE, BECAUSE OF ALL THE HEAVY OIL RIGS, THE LAND IS INCLINED TO BE A BIT MORESO THESE DAYS.

97

MARK WHEELER

98

...and now another chapter in the continuing saga of:
"GOIL & BOYL"

(TWO DROPS OF PRUDHOE BAY OIL)

CHAPTER SEVEN:
"VALDEZ, VALDEZ HERE WE COME... MAYBE!"

ONCE UPON A TUNDRA...

THERE WERE TWO HAPPY DROPS OF OIL. THEY WERE VERY OLD AND DIDN'T GET MANY VISITORS.

ONE DAY THEY HEARD FOOTSTEPS OVERHEAD AS IF IN THE APARTMENT UPSTAIRS BUT THERE WASN'T ANY APARTMENT UP THERE, BUT, NEVER-THE-LESS THE FOOTSTEPS COULD STILL BE HEARD... THEN VOICES!

ONE VOICE SAID,"COME OUT OF THERE WITH YOUR OCTANES UP OR WE'RE COMING DOWN TO GET YOU!" ALL OF A SUDDEN

THE TWO DROPS FELT THE BITE OF A BIT. THE BIT BIT THE DRIPS AND THE DRIPS BIT THE BIT BACK. BAFFLED BY THE BITING AND BITTER, THEY WERE, ALAS, BEATEN.

THE DRIPS HAD BEEN BAGGED AND WERE PUT INTO VARIOUS PIPES (BAG PIPES THEY BEMOANED) WITHOUT EVEN A MAP OR A COMPASS.

THEY TRAVELED FOR DAYS AND DAYS AND THEY BEGAN TO FEEL

WARMER AND WARMER. THE WARMER THEY BECAME, THE MORE THEY FELT THE NEED FOR A COLD DRINK. THEY BOTH LIKED WINE, MAINLY PORT, WHICH THEY ALWAYS DRANK WITH ICE IN PORT FLIPS (AND GOT "GASSED").

ALL OF A SUDDEN THEY SAW A SIGN THAT SAID,"WELCOME TO VALDEZ...ICE...FREE PORT."

THE DROPS WERE VERY HAPPY AND LIVED THAT WAY UNTIL THEY LANDED ON YOUR DRIVEWAY.

99

A LIST OF STUFF YOU JUST MIGHT LIKE TO KNOW ABOUT **VALDEZ** (EVEN IF YOU LIVE THERE)

VALDEZ IS PRONOUNCED, "VAL-DEEZ".
VALDEZ IS IN ALASKA.
VALDEZ HAS ITS VERY OWN ZIP CODE.
VALDEZ IS AN "ICY FREEPORT."
VALDEZ HAS AT LEAST SIX OFFICIAL NICKNAMES.
VALDEZ IS WITHIN THE SOUND OF PRINCE WILLIAM.
VALDEZ IS BOTH THE 2nd OLDEST AND THE NEWEST CITY IN ALASKA.
VALDEZ HAS THE FINEST CAMPGROUNDS IN THE STATE.

MARK WHEELER

*A record snowfall of 975 inches (height of an eight story building) was established near Valdez.*

## VALDEZ

Valdez (Val-deez) is getting its name in the papers quite often these days. Everybody in town is thinking of oil and everybody is checking everybody else's hands trying to find a greasy palm.

When speaking of Valdez you have to distinguish between Valdez B.E. (Before Earthquake), and Valdez A.E. (After Earthquake). Valdez was very hard hit during the big quake and they had to move the whole town four miles from where it was B.E.

Now Valdez A.E. is also Valdez B.O. (Before Oil) and it is not certain right now what will happen with the pipeline. Although it is not sure what the future will bring, everyone knows what the pipeline will bring . . . besides oil.

Regardless of what happens Valdez will remain as the Gateway to the Interior and the Northernmost Ice-Free Port in Alaska.

100

*"If the pipeline doesn't get approved, Valdez will have the best water, sewer and downspout system in Alaska!"*

MARK WHEELER

101

DEED

MARK WHEELER

## PRUDHOE BAY

Now we present Prudhoe Bay where all the oil is supposed to be. A lot of folks have been working very hard up there and a whole bunch of scientists, environmentalists, oil executives, workers, arctic foxes, and caribou, are most anxious to see how things are going to work out.

Oil is pretty basic stuff to our way of life these days. In a way it's pretty good that it is up there and not in downtown San Francisco or in Glacier National Park or under the Empire State Building.

The oil companies are to be commended for their efforts to preserve the ecological balance in the tundra, and although the area will probably never be seen by any but a miniscule percentage of the world's population, it is still nice to know of the conservation efforts being practiced.

*There are a third more men in Alaska than women.*

"I WISH THEY WOULD DECIDE ON THE PIPELINE PRETTY SOON... MY ARMS ARE TIRED!"

MARK WHEELER

# NORTHERN LIGHTS:
"NORTHERN" (PERTAINS TO THE RAILROADS USING THE WORD IN THEIR NAMES) AND "LIGHTS" (LIKE THE ONES THOMAS EDISON INVENTED AND WHICH NOW ARE ON THE FRONT OF THOSE TRAINS) SO "NORTHERN LIGHTS" ARE THE LIGHTS ON THE FRONTS OF THOSE TRAINS.

103

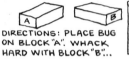

**HERE ARE SOME WAYS TO AVOID GETTING EATEN ALIVE BY LITTLE BUGS:**

YOU CAN USE A SPECIAL ALASKAN INSECT REPELLANT:

* AF-35° IS ANTI-FREEZE GOOD TO -35° F.

ALASKAN ANTI-BUG STUFF WITH AF-35°

DIRECTIONS: NORTH, EAST WEST, & SOUTH

OR YOU CAN USE THIS SPECIAL BUG MASHER:

DIRECTIONS: PLACE BUG ON BLOCK "A". WHACK HARD WITH BLOCK "B"...

OR YOU CAN MAKE THIS SPECIAL BUG BOMB HAT RIG:

OR YOU CAN JUST TRY TO COEXIST WITH THE LITTLE NASTIES (DID SOMEONE CALL THEM "LITTLE"?)

SPECIAL NOTICE: IF YOU SPOT ANYBODY GETTING KIDNAPPED BY A MOSQUITO PLEASE CALL THE AIR FORCE OR YOUR LOCAL ALASKA STATE TROOPER...

## NO-SEE-UMS

No-See-Ums are bugs you can't see. Sometimes you can hear them but you won't see 'em. If you can see them you have two choices as to what to do with your rare talent. Call either the circus where you can be a side show attraction or call your neighborhood psychiatric hospital where you can be a patient for observation.

*No-See-Ums are also called "Punkies."*

**NO-SEE-UM:** *

SEE SIX VARIETIES ILLUSTRATED ON NEXT PAGE

USUALLY (NOT) SEEN IN THE PLURAL, BETTER YET IN THE MULTI-PLURAL. ALTHOUGH YOU CAN'T SEE THEM, THEY CAN SEE YOU, AT LEAST WELL ENOUGH TO MAKE A MEAL OUT OF YOUR ARM OR LEG.

* NO-SEE-UMS ARE CALLED MANY DIFFERENT THINGS, MOSTLY UNPRINTABLE...

104

I CAN'T DRAW
WHAT I CAN'T SEE...

*An Alaskan No-See-Um.*

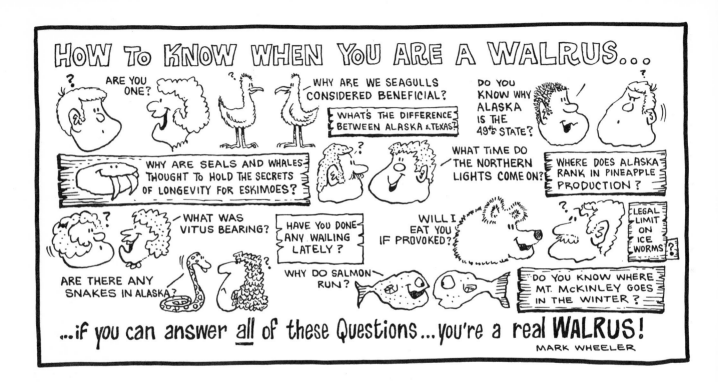

HOW TO KNOW WHEN YOU ARE A WALRUS...

ARE YOU ONE?

WHY ARE WE SEAGULLS CONSIDERED BENEFICIAL?

WHAT'S THE DIFFERENCE BETWEEN ALASKA & TEXAS?

DO YOU KNOW WHY ALASKA IS THE 49th STATE?

WHY ARE SEALS AND WHALES THOUGHT TO HOLD THE SECRETS OF LONGEVITY FOR ESKIMOES?

WHAT TIME DO THE NORTHERN LIGHTS COME ON?

WHERE DOES ALASKA RANK IN PINEAPPLE PRODUCTION?

WHAT WAS VITUS BEARING?

HAVE YOU DONE ANY WAILING LATELY?

WILL I EAT YOU IF PROVOKED?

LEGAL LIMIT ON ICE WORMS?

ARE THERE ANY SNAKES IN ALASKA?

WHY DO SALMON RUN?

DO YOU KNOW WHERE MT. McKINLEY GOES IN THE WINTER?

...if you can answer all of these Questions...you're a real WALRUS!

MARK WHEELER

106

## WALRUS

There are two different kinds of walrus in Alaska. One is the familiar sea animal variety which is a member of the seal family. The other looks more human-like and may be a member of your family. In fact if you are a tourist on your second trip, you might already be a walrus and not even know it.

The sea-type walrus is perhaps best known for its marvelous ivory tusks which can be seen protruding from its upper jaw. These tusks are not only good for digging but make excellent two-hole punches too. These walrus also have funny mustaches and a thick layer of fat (called blubber) all over their bodies. Although some of the human-variety walrus might have mustaches, to have any of the other physical characteristics would render a person quite unbecoming, except of course, to another walrus. The only similarity between a walrus and a person is the fact that when asked if one is a walrus, both should give the same answer.

*An igloo divided against itself will not stand.*

107

## TOURISTS' QUESTIONS

As a tourist, see how many of these clever questions you can answer on Alaska:

1. What was *Vitus Bering* bearing?
2. How many mushes moves a malemute?
3. What time is the seal show?
4. Where are tickets sold for the *Aurora Borealis* show?
5. Who was *John Barrow*?
6. What is the protein content of blubber?
7. What's the difference between goose up and goose down?
8. Why can't you walk on either *muskeg* or *muskox* very well?
9. Why should you become a walrus?
10. What are the *Blue Canoes*?
11. What is the difference between a *glacier* and a *glazier*?
12. Why were the Russians thought to be *Orthodox*?
13. Why does gold get rushed?
14. What does a *No-see-um* look like?
15. Is *your* igloo warm?
16. What are the differences between Kodak and Polaroid bears?

108

In 1946 Alaskans voted for statehood 9,630 to 6,822.

"TiPS FOR TiPPiTY TRAVELLERS:"

HERE ARE SEVEN REALLY INTERESTING THINGS YOU'LL WISH YOU KNEW BEFORE:

1. YOU CAN ACTUALLY USE REAL UNITED STATES MONEY IN ALASKA!
2. SAME GOES FOR STAMPS!
3. YOU DON'T NEED A SPECIAL PASSPORT TO GO FROM KETCHIKAN TO BARROW.
4. IF YOU'RE FROM THE U.S. YOU HAVE THE SAME PRESIDENT AND CONGRESS AS ALL ALASKA.
5. NOT ALL ALASKANS ARE FUR TRAPPERS AND/OR GOLD PANNERS.
6. NOT ALL ALASKANS EAT BLUBBER.
7. MOST ALASKANS ARE U.S. CITIZENS.

*"This wouldn't fit in my luggage so I thought I'd mail it home..."*

109

ASTRO DOME
UNIVERSITY OF HOUSTON
NASA MANNED SPACECRAFT CENTER
ALASKA
GAS - FOOD - SOME LODGING ~ NEXT EXIT

MARK WHEELER

**OUTSIDE:**

"OUT" IS THE SAME AS EXIT OR THE STATE OF BEING THE OPPOSITE OF IN. "SIDE" IS LIKE OF BEEF. "OUTSIDE" IS A DIRECTIONAL COMMAND TO A COW OR STEER. THE TERM USUALLY IS USED IN REFERENCE TO THE WHITE AREAS ON THE MAP:

*The Northern Lights (Aurora Borealis) have no Texan counterparts.*

## OUTSIDE

This word is probably one of the most confusing terms used in Alaska. As a salesman I had an appointment in Anchorage and spent about 10 days and $700 to get there at the appointed time and date, only to be told my customer was "outside," to which I almost replied, "Why don't you go outside and get him." Outside means anywhere except Alaska.

...a peek at the rousing battle between Alaska & Texas...(round 9):

**ALASKA** IS NOW THE BIGGEST STATE IN THE U.S.A. HAS MORE POLAR BEARS...HAS BIG TALL MOUNTAINS...HAS MORE OIL WELLS...HAS MORE ISLANDS... HAS MORE ALASKANS PLUS SOME TEXANS...HAS MORE FERRY BOATS... HAS MORE SAND (UNDERWATER)... HAS MORE SALMON...HAS MORE PERMAFROST...

*VS: *"VS" MEANS, "VERY WELL MIGHT SNICKER AT..."

**TEXAS** ISN'T THE BIGGEST STATE ANY MORE... HAS RATTLE SNAKES...HAS OIL WELLS... IS ON THE GULF OF MEXICO...HAS LESS RAIN...HAS MORE TEXANS... HAS MORE PEOPLE...HAS MORE CACTUS...HAS MORE SAND DUNES... HAS MORE TALL BUILDINGS...HAS MORE PALM TREES...HAS MORE BILLBOARDS...

MARK WHEELER

111

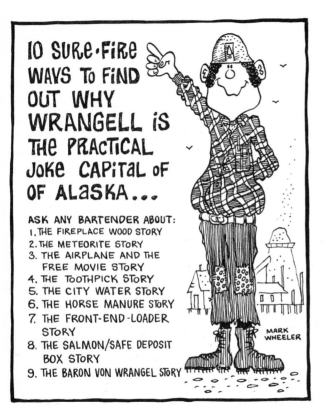

10 SURE-FIRE WAYS TO FIND OUT WHY WRANGELL IS THE PRACTICAL JOKE CAPITAL OF OF ALASKA...

ASK ANY BARTENDER ABOUT:
1. THE FIREPLACE WOOD STORY
2. THE METEORITE STORY
3. THE AIRPLANE AND THE FREE MOVIE STORY
4. THE TOOTHPICK STORY
5. THE CITY WATER STORY
6. THE HORSE MANURE STORY
7. THE FRONT-END-LOADER STORY
8. THE SALMON/SAFE DEPOSIT BOX STORY
9. THE BARON VON WRANGEL STORY

MARK WHEELER

## WRANGELL

Traveling further north (and/or south) take a minute to visit Wrangell (some have done it in less than 45 seconds).

If anyone asks, you don't pronounce the "W," just like you don't pronounce the "L" in salmon. Wrangell, the city, has something to do with Wrangel, the Siberian Island, mainly because the Russians at one time owned both.

In 1834 the Russians built a fort to keep out the Hudson's Bay Company. The city fathers could have refused to give the Bay a business license but they thought if there was a fort in the deal, why not?

Then in 1867 the United States built a military post. Too bad Wrangell already had an abundance of civilian posts and nobody knew what to do with them either.

*"I just tried to call the Chamber of Commerce about that but the operator says their new number is unlisted!"*

113

# EVERYTHING THERE IS TO KNOW ABOUT PARKAS:

A PARKA IS LIKE AN OUTER GARMENT. THIS GARMENT IS USUALLY MADE FROM FURS WHICH THE ANIMALS KNOW TO BE WINDPROOF. APPARENTLY WHAT IS GOOD FOR THE ANIMALS IS GOOD ENOUGH FOR MAN. PARKAS ARE WORN OVER WHAT EVER ELSE YOU'RE WEARING INCLUDING ANY (OR ALL) OF THE FOLLOWING SUITS:

BIRTHDAY.
SUNDAY BEST.
SWIM.
JACKS, CLUBS, HEARTS, & SPADES.
OR ARMOR.

MAN WEARING PARKA WHICH WAS MADE FOR A MUCH TALLER MAN BUT NO TALLER MODEL WAS AVAILABLE...

MARK WHEELER

114

# PARKA:

"PARKA" IS A CONTRACTION. THE PHRASE IS, "WHYA DONNA YOU PARKA DA CAR OVA' DER?"

## PALMER

Almost every tourist and native alike has seen photographs (at least) of those gigantic vegetables grown in the Matanuska Valley just north of Anchorage. Palmer is the headquarters for the Valley and most of the people there grow all those radishes and cabbages. The people from Palmer are recognizable by their big green thumbs.

*Chickens in Alaska produce the second fewest eggs in the country.*

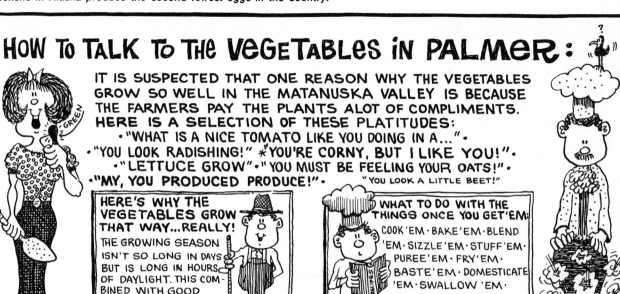

# HOW TO TALK TO THE VEGETABLES IN PALMER:

IT IS SUSPECTED THAT ONE REASON WHY THE VEGETABLES GROW SO WELL IN THE MATANUSKA VALLEY IS BECAUSE THE FARMERS PAY THE PLANTS ALOT OF COMPLIMENTS. HERE IS A SELECTION OF THESE PLATITUDES:

• "WHAT IS A NICE TOMATO LIKE YOU DOING IN A..." •
• "YOU LOOK RADISHING!" * YOU'RE CORNY, BUT I LIKE YOU!" •
• "LETTUCE GROW" • "YOU MUST BE FEELING YOUR OATS!" •
• "MY, YOU PRODUCED PRODUCE!" •     "YOU LOOK A LITTLE BEET!"

HERE'S WHY THE VEGETABLES GROW THAT WAY... REALLY!
THE GROWING SEASON ISN'T SO LONG IN DAYS BUT IS LONG IN HOURS OF DAYLIGHT. THIS COMBINED WITH GOOD SOIL DOES IT!

WHAT TO DO WITH THE THINGS ONCE YOU GET 'EM:
COOK 'EM · BAKE 'EM · BLEND 'EM · SIZZLE 'EM · STUFF 'EM · PUREE 'EM · FRY 'EM · BASTE 'EM · DOMESTICATE 'EM · SWALLOW 'EM ·

* ACTUALLY CORN, NOT LIKING THAT REMARK, DOESN'T GROW SO HOT.

MARK WHEELER

115

REMEMBER THE GOLD RUSH?

"At 40° below . . . in Nome . . . what else? Have 'nuther one. . ."

MARK WHEELER

116

## NOME

Nome is on the range that is referred to in the song "Nome on the Range." Being built entirely on permafrost it looks like a carpenter's nightmare in spots and the town could use some plumb bobs and some plumbing (indoors).

A new variety of Gold Fever (unlike Klondikeitus) plagued the town in 1898. It was called Panitonthebeachitus. Over 20,000 hardy souls had had it when the rush became less so. Today a few thousand folks live there and they are called "Gnomes" because they all live very close to the ground.

Nome has a native hospital and a very curious sanitation system which would require a whole book to explain.

Nome was leveled by a fire in 1934 and that took care of it horizontally but vertically it is still somewhat out of whack.

# PERMAFROST:

"PERMA" IS THE FIRST PART OF "PERMANENT" WHICH MEANS "FOR GOOD" AND "FROST" IS THE CONDITION WHEN DEW AND OTHER AIRBORNE MOISTURE ARE FROZEN, HENCE "PERMAFROST" ASKS THE QUESTION, "WHAT GOOD IS FROZEN?"

*Over half the state is on permafrost.*

"SORRY I FORGOT TO TELL YOU NOT TO STAND IN ONE PLACE ON PERMAFROST TOO LONG WHEN YOU'RE WEARING THOSE ELECTRIC SOX!"

MARK WHEELER

117

WHAT EVERY WELL-EQUIPPED ESKIMO HUNTER NEEDS TO HUNT WITH:

I'M WELL RIGGED!

MARK WHEELER

AN OOMIAK: THAT IS A SKIN BOAT WHICH IS VERY HANDY WHEN TRAVELLING OVER WATER...

A LASSO: VERY GOOD UNLESS GAME IS OUT OF RANGE OR UNDER-WATER, ETC.

A RIFLE: MAY BE USED INSTEAD OF A LASSO. ALSO CAN BE EFFECTIVE OVER LONGER DISTANCES.

A SPEAR OR HARPOON: ABSOLUTELY A MUST!

GOOD EYES: VERY BASIC TO GOOD HUNTING.

A SPY GLASS: TO BE USED WITH ONE GOOD EYE!

A SNOW MACHINE: FAST REPLACING DOG TEAMS FOR ARCTIC TRAVEL... GRRR!

A HELICOPTER: THOUGH NOT AVAILABLE TO ALL CAN'T BE BEAT FOR SOME!

Poke:

"OINK...OINK!"

* THIS IS A PIG IN A POKE...

*The Arctic Coastal Plain is very plain.*

## ESKIMO HUNTING

Eskimos are known world over for their excellent abilities as hunters. An eskimo can hide from game so well that more seals, walrus, and polar bears die of fright than any other cause. Most eskimos hunt for food and clothing about the same way we go shopping. The basic difference is that the eskimo goes hunting mainly out of necessity rather than for status. . .

118

WHY YOU SHOULD keep a KEEN EYE ON KENAi...

LOOKiNG CLOSER WE FIND KENAI HAS A WHOLE BUNCH OF:

- OIL
- GAS (NATURALLY)
- RUNNING SALMON
- NEW BUILDINGS
- DOCKS · PIERS · ETC.
- INVESTMENT OPPORTUNITIES
- ROOM TO EXPAND
- SHOPPING PLACES
- NICE PEOPLE
- FERTILIZER
- REFINERY STUFF
- PAVED ROADS
- MOOSE
- FINE MOUNTAIN SCENERY
- ACTIVE VOLCANOES NEARBY
- DRILLING PLATFORMS
- AIRPORT SPACE
- FAST GROWING SUBURBS

MARK WHEELER

*Oil was discovered on the Kenai Peninsula on January 19, 1957.*

## KENAI

On the Sterling Highway southwest of Anchorage one can't help but bump into Kenai. Again the Russians, now long famous for discovering places, added Kenai to their list in 1791. But, lucky for future generations, the practice of naming places with unpronounceable names was at least suspended for the time being and Kenai was the result.

Oil has almost replaced fishing as an excuse for hanging around there and there is still speculation that Kenai might really boom one day with natural gas. The term "boom" admittedly seems to be a bad choice in this case but nevertheless the investors are still waiting.

If you drive further south from Kenai you should exercise extreme caution as the highway ends there.

119

# SAYINGS, PHRASES, AND BAD JOKES THE PEOPLE IN KENAI ARE GETTING PRETTY (IN FACT, VERY) TIRED OF HEARING:

If you discover Gold, you yell "Eureka!" If you discover Oil, you yell "Arco!"

THERE'S NO FUEL LIKE AN OIL FUEL...

"MY OIL FLAME IS BACK HOME IN OKLAHOMA!"

"OIL FRIENDS ARE NOT SOON FORGOTTEN."

A FUEL AND HIS MONEY ARE SOON PARTED...

"THAT OIL GANG OF MINE."

OIL WILL GIVE YOU A NEW LEASE ON LIFE

No matter how Humble... There's no place like Home! (EVEN IF IT'S A MOBIL HOME...)

MARK WHEELER

"ISAT YOUR RIG?"

"OIL BE WITH YOU IN APPLE BLOSSOM TIME."

WHAT'S ALL THIS WILD CHATTER ABOUT WILD CATTERS?

"I don't care whose dog you are, stop watchin' me like that!" (SORRY ENCO)

"OIL BE DARNED!"

GIVE ME THAT OIL SOFT SHOE... (WHATA GAS!)

120

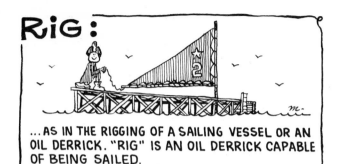

# RiG:

...AS IN THE RIGGING OF A SAILING VESSEL OR AN OIL DERRICK. "RIG" IS AN OIL DERRICK CAPABLE OF BEING SAILED.

## RIG

The word "Rig" as used in Alaska is just one more term about which there is much confusion. A rig is not necessarily an oil rig but can be if so desired. A rig in Alaska can be any object from a car to a sled to a truck, boat, airplane, or jar of peanut butter. One who fools around with such stuff is called a "rigger" (also may be called a "fool").

## WHY iT iS SUCH A GaS To ViSiT aND/OR LiVe iN KeNai, ALaSKa:

1. YOU CAN WATCH THE OIL EXECUTIVES RUNNING AROUND POINTING THEIR FINGERS AND SAYING, "WELL, WELL...WELL."
2. YOU CAN LISTEN TO THE OIL TOWER (PLATFORM) PEOPLE ROWING ASHORE SINGING, "OIL SOL 'AMIO..."
3. YOU CAN FEEL THE EXCITEMENT WHEN PEOPLE TALK ABOUT THE NATURAL GAS BOOM...

OiL See YOU iN KENAi...

4. YOU CAN GET THE FEELING OF LIVING LIKE A GOLD FISH AS ALL THE INVESTORS WAIT.
5. YOU CAN COMPARE THE OIL COMPANIES CLAIMS OF ENVIRONMENTAL PROTECTION WITH THE DEPARTMENT OF INTERIOR'S STATEMENTS.
6. YOU CAN TALK ABOUT OIL WITH A MOOSE.
7. YOU HELP THE OIL PEOPLE SPEND THEIR MONEY!
8. YOU CAN ENCOURAGE PEOPLE TO DRIVE AROUND ALOT.

121

*"Well, you get the daily prize anyway. . ."*

122

# SALMON:

"SAL" IS FROM SALAMI AND "MON" LIKE IN MONDAY COMBINES TO SALMON WHICH IS A SALAMI YOU EAT ONLY ON MONDAYS.

## SALMON

Salmon are caught in nets by two main methods: Purse Seining and Trolling. In Purse Seining the fish are snatched out of the water (called "Purse Snatching") whereas in Trolling they are caught with the help of special people (called "Trols") who have the ability to wander about to get just the fish they want. Note of interest: Fish net and Alaska mosquito net both have the same sized holes.

MOST OF THE QUESTIONS YOU'VE ALWAYS WANTED TO ASK A SALMON (IF YOU EVER MET ONE FACE-TO-FACE OR ELSEWHERE):

1. WHERE EXACTLY ARE YOU GOING TO BE AT SALMON DERBY TIME?
2. WHAT DO YOU LIKE TO EAT?
3. WHAT IS YOUR FAVORITE COLOR?
4. ARE THERE ANY MORE AT HOME LIKE YOU?
5. WOULD YOU LIKE TO HAVE YOUR PICTURE IN THE NEWSPAPER? ...ON T.V.? ...IN SOME BROCHURES?
6. DO YOU WANT TO HANG ON THE WALL AT MY HOUSE OR DOWN AT THE CHAMBER OF COMMERCE?

123

## WHY ALASKANS HAVE SO MUCH PRIDE IN THE INSIDE STUFF IN ALASKA:

1. SINCE THE WEATHER GOVERNS SO MUCH, THE QUEST FOR BASIC NEEDS (FOOD, SHELTER, CLOTHING) IS THAT MUCH TOUGHER.

2. A BIG BUNCH OF FOLKS HAVE BUILT THEIR OWN HOMES AND HAVE PIONEER-ED ALASKA.

3. THE REMOTENESS OF THE VILLAGES MAKES THINGS COST MUCH MORE THAN IN THE "LOWER-48."

4. ALASKANS DO NOT LIKE LAZY PEOPLE.

MARK WHEELER

*More Alaskans are "natives" than were born there.*

TO CONTINUE OUR EDUCATIONAL PROGRAM ON THE BEHALF OF THE SALMON WE NOW GIVE YOU THE DETAIL OF DE TAIL:

ALASKAN SALMON

## SIWASH:

"SI" (PRONOUNCED "SYE") IS A PART OF "SIZE", AND "WASH" IS WHAT YOU DO AT THE LAUNDROMAT ON SATURDAYS. "SIWASH?" IS LIKE ASKING, "WHAT SIZE IS YOUR WASH?"

WHAT HAS THIS GOT TO DO WITH ALASKA?

124

"A couple of weeks ago that fish could've jumped up there all by himself..."

MARK WHEELER

125

*"I think I've found your power problem. . ."*

MARK WHEELER

126

## SLED DOGS AND DOGGEREL

It's some wonder all sled dogs don't have neuroses requiring professional help. What would you think if you had to answer to four or five different names? Names like, "Husky, Malamute, Sled Dog, Man's best friend, and/or Mush." All of these names are designed to put on the dog as it were, but to the dogs it just adds to the confusion.

It is certainly lucky for man that sled dogs don't write letters or talk on the phone. If they did they might learn how the dogs in the hills of Kentucky live or about the dog eat dog world of our metropolitan areas.

Thanks to the snowmobile, to live a dog's life in Alaska may again become less difficult in the near future. But, speaking of snowmobiles, many sled dogs are forming a coalition to lobby for equal opportunity employment. At last check the dogs were getting ready to form a blockade of solid dogs parallel to the Dew Line and not allow any snowmobiles across the line.

The dogs plan to carry the battle right to the top of the pile and continue to push (rather than pull) for equal rights.

If all that were not enough, the dogs also plan to lobby for softer harnesses, shorter hours, more fringe benefits, higher pensions, and earlier retirement plus bonus incentives to participate in the Anchorage Fur Rendezvous World Championship Dog Sled Races (AFRWCDSR or ARF for short). The resolution of the problem seems to be not to treat sled dogs like dogs.

A GOOD DOG TEAM CAN WHIZ ALONG AT 15 MPH OVER GOOD COUNTRY (FLAT, WITH A BIT OF HARD SNOW ON IT).

HERE IS THE LAST WORD IN A.T.V.'s (ALL TERRAIN VEHICLES). IT IS A SPIFFY COMBINATION OF AIRPLANE, OFF-THE-ROAD TRAIL BIKE, NEWSPAPER DELIVERER, MOOSE CHASER, GOLF CART, AND OTHER STUFF!

# SLED DOG:

SPECIAL BREED OF DOG (CALLED A "MALAMUSH" OR "PHIDAUX") WITH, INSTEAD OF FOUR FEET, MINIATURE SKIS OR RUNNERS ON THE BOTTOM TO HELP HIM TRAVEL ON ALL THE SNOW.

## SNOWMOBILES

Snowmobiles are really popular in Alaska, much to the dismay of the sled dogs. We heard about one enterprising fellow caught between the new fangled mechanical machine and the dogs he loved so much.

Faced with the problem of exercising his dogs he turned his snowmobile upside down, turned it on, and let his dogs run on the moving track.

The idea worked great until the dog started thinking he was a squirrel and began to run around gathering nuts which he hid in a cache, all the while mumbling something about the coming of winter. . .

## YOU CAN LAUNCH A BILLION SNOWBALLS AT ONE TIME ON YOUR UPSIDE DOWN SNOWMOBILE...

*There is a snowmobile race in February over the 260 miles from Anchorage to Fairbanks.*

128

"... and this one was owned by a little old lady from Pasadena..."

MARK WHEELER

129

*"OK fellow legislators, let's call this caucus to order . . . BARTENDER!"*

130

## JUNEAU

Juneau is the capital of the State of Alaska, a fact which says nothing about the state of Juneau at any particular time. When the legislature is in session a state of confusion prevails and some of the legislators get themselves in various states simultaneously.

Juneau was named for Joe Juneau who, with Richard Harris, was out looking for a good time. Obviously one of them must have had a better time than the other because the place is not named Harrisburg, or Harrisville, or even Harris City.

Originally Sitka was the capital but one night the people from Juneau built a capitol building and then sent a moving van over to load up the political machine, a couple of bureaus, and some slow-moving wheels the government had.

Now Juneau is the official capital of Alaska which is more than can be said about Juneau, Wisconsin.

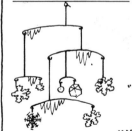

WHERE TO GO CAMERA CLICKING IN AND AROUND JUNEAU... MENDENHALL GLACIER · MENDENHALL LAKE · GASTINEAU CHANNEL · ALASKA JUNEAU MINE (WHAT'S LEFT) · THE HOUSE OF WICKERSHAM · ALASKA STATE HISTORICAL MUSEUM · RED DOG S'LOON · ALL THE STATUES & MONUMENTS · RUSSIAN ORTHODOX CHURCH · THE "OLD WITCH" TOTEM · THE CAPITOL BUILDING · THE MILLION DOLLAR GOLF COURSE · ETC.

SNOWMOBILE: A MOBILE IS A PIECE OF ART THAT HANGS FROM THE CEILING (SEA SEALING, NO RELATION) AND MOVES IN THE BREEZE AND A "SNOWMOBILE" IS SIMPLY A MOBILE MADE FROM SNOW. (HARD TO BUILD IN THE SPRING AND SUMMER)

MARK WHEELER

131

THE VOYAGEUR

Half Baked Alaska BY MARK WHEELER

...if you don't see it...we'll order it!

MARK WHEELER

"The author bounced in here one day and wanted to sell some paintings, then some sketches, then some prints and then, finally he came out with a book!"

132

## KETCHIKAN

And now we come to Ketchikan, otherwise known as the, "Salmon Capital of the World," and "The Gateway to Alaska," and "The First City of Alaska."

Ketchikan probably has more stairs than any other town (except maybe Juneau) which makes it very easy to get to work (watch for banister splinters) but very hard to get back home.

In the old days Ketchikan was a ruckus place with a lot of singing, dancing, and carrying on but, as of last week, things have quieted down. Creek Street was the center for a lot of activities that are now illegal but if buildings talked, Creek Street might get arrested for violation of the Intimate Secrets Act.

Ketchikan is on an island whose name is unpronounceable. It's called Revillagigedo. Actually the man's name was Don Juan Vicenta Güemes Pacheco de Padilla, Count of Rivella Gigedo, Viceroy of New Spain, Registered Voter, Namer of Güemes Island in the San Juans in Washington State, and Leader of all Don Juans.

Deer Mountain is a mainly rocky mountain right behind Ketchikan. Tongass Narrows is a mainly cold water channel right in front of Ketchikan. Ketchikan is between the two.

WHY YOU COULDN'T ASK FOR A MUCH NEATER PLACE THAN KETCHIKAN:

YOU CAN LIVE SO MUCH HISTORY BY: VISITING ANYONE OR PLACES LIKE: CREEK STREET, INDIAN TOWN, TONGASS HISTORICAL MUSEUM, TOTEM PARK, SAXMAN, THE CEREMONIAL HOUSE, BAR HARBOR, THOMAS BASIN, ANY BAR, THE FIRESIDE

I'M A FAN

*Ketchikan has no yellow elephants.*

## SOURDOUGH:

1. USED BY BEARS TO DESCRIBE THE TASTE WHEN EATING HUNTERS WITH MONEY IN THEIR POCKETS.
2. TO LABEL A PERSON WHO IS SOUR ON ALASKA BUT AIN'T GOT THE DOUGH TO GET OUT.

MARK WHEELER

133

IF YOU THINK
**MEYERS CHUCK**
is a FUNNY NaMe, CHeCK OUT ALL
THeSe OTHeR iNTeReSTiNG ReaL PLaCeS:

(ALL ACTUAL REAL PLACES TOO)

| NAME | ZIP CODE |
|------|----------|
| CHUKFAKTOOLIK | 99559 |
| KWINHAGAK | 99655 |
| MARY'S IGLOO | 99778 |
| HONOLULU | * |
| IGIUGIG | 99613 |
| OUZINKIE | 99644 |
| KEPANGALOOK | 99559 |
| HOUSTON | |
| MONTANA | |
| WEST POINT | |
| CAPE ATUSHGAVIK | |
| LAKE CHAKACKAMNA | |
| CHUGINADAK ISLAND | |
| REVILLAGIGEDO ISLAND | |

MARK WHEELER   * NOW ABANDONED

The per capita booze consumption statewide is the highest in the country.

## MEYERS CHUCK

Meyers Chuck is not a stop on the Alaska Marine Highway nor is it much of a tourist mecca at all. At one time there was a plan to issue a very fancy brochure to all the travel agents in the world showing Meyers Chuck to be (a) bigger than Anchorage, (b) more prosperous than Kenai, (c) more picturesque than Valdez, and (d) offer better hunting than Kodiak. The plan had to be abandoned though when it was discovered that the Chamber of Commerce was not only short on funds but didn't even exist.

All this doesn't leave Meyers Chuck without a claim to fame. Meyers Chuck is the Home Brew capital of Alaska. Local folks call it, "Sun Tan Lotion, Paint Remover, Fiberglass Catalyst or Sinus Congestion Remover," and the high octane stuff is guaranteed to stop high blood pressure and/or a palpitating heart.

If you are going into Meyers Chuck be sure you take a boat or plane but don't take a black briefcase or even a clipboard. If you work for the government, don't mention it and if you are a "revenooer" disregard all of the above, and stay out of town.

134

*". . . and my product will give you a rosy glow even if you don't go out in the sun."*

135

"Oh yes, you've stayed with us before haven't you Mr. Baranof?"

136

# SITKA

Alexander Baronof probably named Sitka. In those days the Russians used the suffix "ka" on lots of ordinary words like "vod" and "alas" so it seemed to fit right in.

Sitka is one of the older towns in Alaska by the fact that it was founded around 1799 and was the capital of Russian-America after the crabs invaded Kodiak. Sitka was the capital for 68 years. In 1802 Baronof and the Tlingit Indians had words and the Tlingits held a big massacre which, unfortunately, many Russians attended thinking it was a birthday party for Peter the Great. It was quite a party and in 1804, the Russians rebuilt the town after waiting two years for their loan to get approved. After that Baronof treated the Tlingits a bit more like first class citizens because he knew when he was outnumbered.

Today Sitka couldn't be more picturesque. The town even has a back yard volcano right where the barbecue should be. Luckily they let Mt. Edgecumbe become extinct before they snuggled up too close to it.

Sitka has the famous Russian Orthodox Church, rebuilt now after the original burned, and has its very own bus. (Hello Gene!), a distinction shared with Ketchikan (Hello George and Ollie) and a very few other Alaskan towns.

If you order Russian Salad Dressing you can get a better idea of the flavor of the area. Naturally the Russians did more than make salad dressing and evidence of this can be found in the excellent museum and mementos every place you look, especially at the Centennial Building.

SOURDOUGHS SAY: SEE SIZZLIN' SITKA BY THE SEA! THEN WRITE TO THE STATE FERRY SYSTEM AND GET THEM TO GET SITKA A BETTER FERRY SCHEDULE!

## TERMINATION DUST

Given to eloquence, Alaskans even have a special term for Termination Dust. It is called "snow." The reason for the word snow is that it describes what the stuff is better and it combines with other words better too. Who's ever heard of a "Termination Dust Mobile" or a "Termination Dust Shovel"? Since a stranded person is said to be "snowed in" it makes sense to say that instead of "Termination Dusted."

## PRINCE RUPERT, CANADA

Prince Rupert was the son of Queen Charlotte and King Salmon. He was born at a very early age before he learned there was a difference between Alaska and Canada, where he lives today. The Alaska Ferries stop by occasionally and bring him a few tourists, and that makes him and his town pretty happy which is approved of by the Queen.

"YOU'LL NEVER GET AWAY WITH USING SNOW FOR LAND FILL!"

MARK WHEELER

TERMINATION DUST: "TERMINATION" IS THE PROCESS YOU GO THROUGH WHEN YOU GET FIRED FROM A JOB AND "DUST" IS WHAT YOU HAVE IN YOUR HOUSE HENCE "TERMINATION DUST" IS DIRT THAT YOU DRAW (OR WRITE) THE WORD "UNEMPLOYMENT" IN. THIS DUST IS USUALLY WHITE.

138

# WHAT PRINCE RUPERT WILL DO FOR YOU (BESIDES REMIND YOU THAT YOU'RE IN CANADA):

**TEACH YOU HISTORY:** LIKE HOW THE PLACE WAS STARTED IN 1906

**SHOW YOU WEATHER:** AVERAGES .25 OF AN INCH OF WETNESS EVERY DAY!

**ENTERTAIN YOU:** BEFORE OR AFTER DARK (CANADIAN OR ALASKAN STYLE)

**DEMONSTRATE LOVE:** THE PRINCES & PRINCESSES ARE QUITE FRIENDLY

**OFFER HOSPITALITY:** (SEE ABOVE)

**PREVENT LONELINESS:** (SEE BELOW)

**PRODUCE ILLUSIONS:** ABOUT ACTUALLY BEING IN A FOREIGN COUNTRY.

**HEAP ON PLATITUDES:** ABOUT WHAT A NICE (MONEY SPENDING) TOURIST...

**SIMPLIFY YOUR LANGUAGE:** BECAUSE YOU CAN PROBABLY SPEAK CANADIAN NOW...

**GIVE YOU LOQUACITY:** WITH SOME NEW WORDS LIKE; "COLOUR, HARBOUR, ZED" ETC.

**RELAX YOUR TENSIONS:** BY LIVING THE LIFE AS THEY LIVE IT IN PRINCE RUPERT...

**GAIN YOU FRIENDS:** NAMELY (AND MAINLY) CANADIANS

**LOSE YOU SOME WEIGHT:** BY JOGGING AROUND TOWN LOOKING AT STUFF...

**HELP YOU SOCIALLY:** YOU'LL NEVER RUN OUT OF CONVERSATION!

**SAVE YOU MONEY:** CANADIAN MONEY CONVERTS AND COMES IN COLOURS...

**KEEP YOU COOL:** AND JUST A WEE BIT DAMP TOO, SOMETIMES...

**GIVE YOU SHALOM:**

MARK WHEELER

*Prince Rupert merchants will take Alaskan money.*

139

*"Take some friendly advice and don't make jokes about loggers."*

MARK WHEELER

140

and now some WORDS 'bout

# LOGGING IN ALASKA

LOGGING HAS A LOT TO DO WITH TREES. TREES GROW IN THE WOODS. IN FACT WITHOUT TREES, THERE WOOD NOT BE ANY WOODS. MOST TREES GROW VERTICALLY, STARTING FROM THE BOTTOM. FROM TREES WE GET TOOTHPICKS, HOUSES, AND, OCCASIONALLY, AN OCCASIONAL LAMP, TABLE, OR CHAIR. WE CAN ALSO GET HURT IF WE BANG INTO ONE WITH OUR CAR (OR BOAT OR AIRPLANE), OR IF ONE FALLS ON US, OR IF WE FALL OFF ONE. SPECIAL NOTE: AFTER A TREE HAS BEEN FELLED IT BECOMES A "LOG" LIKE A SHIP'S LOG OR A PLANES LOG.

MARK WHEELER

*28 million acres of Alaska is commercial timber land.*

## LOGGING

Logging is what you are doing when you are (a) cutting down trees, (b) entering information in a ship's log, (c) flying an airplane (logging time), and/or (e) all of the above at the same time (which is pretty tough). Loggers are known for their funny way of walking (called "lumbering"), and for what they yell when they fall off their bar stools, "Timber. . .!"

# TIMBER CRUISER:

—WHOA!

"TIMBER" IS WHAT YOU ARE SUPPOSED TO YELL WHEN YOU CHOP DOWN A TREE AND A "CRUISER" IS A TYPE OF PLEASURE BOAT HENCE A "TIMBER CRUISER" IS THE CAPTAIN WHO YELLS ALOT WHEN HIS YACHT IS HEADED FOR THE TREES.

141

MARK WHEELER

"Lishen pal . . . ya can't lean against that lamp post all night. . .!"

142

*"You know Horace, we simply **must** get some of these special trees for our north gardens. . ."*

MARK WHEELER

143

HOW TO TELL YOUR AVERAGE TOTEM POLE FROM YOUR AVERAGE TREE:

A TOTEM POLE: STANDS UPRIGHT... HAS ALL KINDS OF CARVING ON IT... USUALLY TELLS A STORY...WAS PROBABLY CARVED BY AN INDIAN...DOES NOT GROW ANYMORE.

A TREE: STANDS UPRIGHT... WON'T TELL YOU A STORY UNLESS YOU CAN HEAR IT... STILL HAS BRANCHES... IS STILL GROWING... MAY BE MADE INTO A HOUSE...OR POLES.

TOTEM POLE:

"TOTE" COMES FROM THE LIKES OF, "TOTE DAT BARGE" - ADD A "M", - AND "POLE" IS WHAT SOMEONE OF POLISH EXTRACTION IS SAID TO BE, HENCE "TOTEM POLE" IS A COMMAND TO GIVE A POLISH SAUSAGE A PIGGY-BACK RIDE. (THIS CAN BE SEEN IN SOUTHEASTERN)

## TOTEM POLES

Many Cheechakoes (ask any Alaskan what the word means) believe that the ornate totem poles grew that way. The rumor spread all over the world and Ladies' Horticultural Societies sent their heartiest members to Alaska to investigate.

The year of this stampede was 1898 which just happened to be the same year that gold was being sought in the Klondike but the gold was incidental to the race for seeds of these special trees.

The women waited and waited but the trees didn't sprout. No buds came, no birds sang, and no ladies got their seeds. All the ladies were furious. They stomped the ground with anger. Their high heels aerated the soil, the rains came, the soil eroded, and all the special trees fell over.

An Indian came along with his ax and began to hack away at the tree. The ladies thought that quite odd, to chop a tree after it already had been felled. They all thought the Indian was crazy and ran away.

144

## ALASKA STATE TREE

The State Tree is the Sitka Spruce. The election was hard fought and some of the other trees campaigned just as hard as the Sitka Spruce. They used all the media available including signs on all the dog sleds, ads in all the papers and an extensive campaign on radio and television, and all the ads used the slogan "The Sitka Spruce is the tree to be."

The Sitka Spruce ran a grass roots campaign through a main trunk office in Sitka (where else) and branch offices all over the State.

DON'T JUST SIT KAROUND, SPRUCE YOUR GARDEN...

*Before statehood there was no state tree.*

WHAT ONE MIGHT FIND HANDY WHEN ONE WISHES TO ATTEMPT TO CARVE A TOTEM POLE:

1. FORMER TREE WHICH HAS BEEN CLEVERLY CONVERTED INTO A HORIZONTAL LOG.
2. A PRETTY SHARP AXE, HATCHET, AND MAYBE A CHISEL.
3. INHERITED TALENT.
4. A LEATHER APRON.
5. A SHARPENING STONE.
6. AN ARTISTIC EYE.
7. A KNOT FINDER.
8. CHALK.
9. TWO SAWHORSES
10. AN UMBRELLA.
11. A CUP OF COFFEE
12. "SIDEWALK SUPERVISORS.
13. A DESIGN PLAN.
14. A CUSTOMER.

"I spotted two hunters coming up the north side . . . let's go get Smokey and his missus, and the cubs, and Wally, Frank, Bill, and Joe, and ambush 'em!"

MARK WHEELER

146

## TRAPPING

The Wildlife Department says there are over 25,000 bears in Alaska alone. If some of them could find a friend there might be a whole lot more.

To trap a bear which might stand fourteen feet tall and weigh more than 70 or 80 Thanksgiving turkeys is no easy job. It takes either a good size trap or an ability to run faster than a disgruntled bear. Both are sometimes required because a bear can uproot a good sized tree (like the one you attached your trap to) and bring it along on the chase, to use later on your head for example. Naturally polar bears won't hit you with a tree but can you dodge a flying iceberg?

More often than not though trappers do not set their traps for bears. It's hard to trap a bear with the right expression on his face for a rug. Lots of other animals are trapped. Bears don't like it. Neither would you.

WHEN TALKING TO A TRAPPER FIRST FIND OUT WHICH KIND OF TRAPPER HE HAS:

ANIMAL TRAP

TRAP AS IN (SHUT YOUR) (SOMETIMES ASSOCIATED WITH A TRAPPER'S WIFE·MATE AND/OR DOG.)

FISH TRAP? TOO BIG & COMPLICATED TO DO PICTURE OF... OR EVEN DRAW.

YE OLDE TRAP DOOR DO NOT OPEN

**TRAPPER:**
A TRAP CAN BE A DEVICE TO CATCH ANIMALS, A PEN TO HOLD FISH, YOUR WIFE'S OR YOUR MOTHER·IN·LAW'S MOUTH, OR THE OPENING ON THE BACKSIDE OF YOUR LONG HANDLED UNDERWEAR. A "TRAPPER" IS A PERSON WHO HAS SOMETHING TO DO WITH ANY ONE (OR ALL) OF THESE TRAPS.
MARK WHEELER

147

MARK WHEELER

"Folks, our next tour will start in just a minute . . . I'm your guide William. . ."

148

## SEWARD

Seward is called "The City of Contrasts" but a better nickname would be "the city of confusion." Just when most ships are ending their voyages there, the Alaska Railroad is just getting started. The ships come and go and the trains do likewise and when they're both gone, there's no town. The only thing that's left is all the scenery and there is a lot of it.

The real claim to fame though are the tremendous iceboxes and follies which are made there. To be the proud owner of a Seward's Icebox or a Seward's Folly is a rare thing indeed as the demand is so much greater than the supply.

SEWARD IS SEAWARD FROM ANCHORAGE...

*Ships transport 90% of goods to and from Alaska.*

WHY SEWARD IS NOT ON THE SEWARD PENINSULA LIKE KENAI IS ON THE KENAI PENINSULA:

SEWARD CAN'T BE FOUND (OR WILL NOT BE FOUND) ON THE SEWARD PENINSULA FOR THE SAME AMBIGUOUS REASON THAT WRANGELL (THE TOWN) IS NO WHERE NEAR WRANGELL (THE MOUNTAIN RANGE) OR THE REASON THAT KODIAK IS ACTUALLY ON KODIAK ISLAND.

TUNDRa:

"TUN" IS A SYLLABLE OF THE WORD "TUNNEL" AND, "DRA" IS FROM THE WORD "DRAFT" WHICH CAN BE AN UNWANTED BREEZE, A KIND OF BEER, A WAY INTO THE ARMY, OR HOW DEEP A BOAT FLOATS. "TUNDRA" MEANS, "UNWANTED, BREEZY, SMOOTH TASTING HOLE IN A MOUNTAIN OWNED BY THE ARMY, THAT IS FLOATING.

MARK WHEELER

149

MARK WHEELER

## HOW TO MAKE A MOUNTAIN OUT OF A MOLE HILL WITH THE VOLCANO METHOD:

TO ACCOMPLISH THIS FRIGHTFUL TASK YOU'LL NEED MOST OF THE INGREDIENTS LISTED ON HERE:

10 TONS - MOLTING (NOT MOLTEN) ROCK
10 TONS - STEAMING LAVA
10 TONS - TERRA FIRMA
A PINCH OF FIRE AND/OR BRIMSTONE

BLEND THE ROCK AND LAVA UNTIL SULPHER FUMES DISAPPEAR, TRY THE FIRMA AND EXTRACT A PINCH OF THE REST. PUT BUTTER ON BURNS.

AND NOW HERE IS A LIST OF MORE OR LESS ACTIVE VOLCANOES IN ALASKA:

TRIDENT VOLCANO
MAKUSHIN VOLCANO
POGROMNI VOLCANO
SHISHALDIN VOLCANO
ILIAMNA VOLCANO
PAVLOF VOLCANO
MAGEIK VOLCANO
KUGAK VOLCANO

THEN THERE IS MT. EDGECUMBE NEAR SITKA... IT USED TO BE A VOLCANO BUT HASN'T ERUPTED LATELY.* *THANK GOODNESS FOR THAT!

*Katmai National Monument is 4,215 sq. miles, Rhode Island is 1,214 sq. miles.*

## VOLCANOES

Volcanoes are actually mountains which are made out of mole hills. Alaska has a pretty complete collection with many in "The Land of the 10,000 Smokes." There used to be less but somebody figured they'd round off the number, which is more than they did for the mountains. To visit a volcano, first distinguish if it's been extinguished.

VOLCANO:

"VOL" IS A CONTRACTION OF "VOLUNTEER" AND "CANO" IS A DERIVITIVE OF "KENO" - A GAME OF CHANCE PLAYED IN LAS VEGAS HENCE "VOLCANO" IS A VOLUNTEER WHO WILL PLAY KENO FOR YOU WITH YOUR MONEY. (IF YOU LOSE, YOU CAN BLOW YOUR TOP!)

151

# SOME OF THE ZILLION THINGS TO DO IN HAINES:

1. TRY TO LIFT A STAWBERRY.
2. FISH FOR FISHES.
3. COUNT ALL THE TREES.
4. PAN FOR GOLD.
5. WATCH THE BIRDIES.
6. EXPERIENCE HIGH & LOW TIDES.
7. CHASE GIRLS.
8. SMELL FRESH VEGE-TABLES.
9. FOLLOW THE OIL PIPE LINE TO FAIRBANKS.
10. CHECK INTO A HOTEL.
11. DRINK BOOZE.
12. DECIDE WHICH FERRY TO TAKE HOME.
13. KISS SOMEONE.

14. VISIT THE INDIANS.
15. HIKE THE DALTON TRAIL.
16. SEE PORT CHILKOOT
17. ENJOY THE CHILKAT DANCERS.
18. CARVE A TOTEM POLE.
19. EAT A SMOKING SALMON.
20. WRESTLE A BEAR.
21. MAKE FRIENDS WITH A TROUT.
22. WALK AROUND
23. SHOOT PICTURES
24. PLAY HOPSCOTCH
25. CHARTER A PLANE
26. HUNT A GOOSE

27. PLAY FOOTSIE WITH A MOOSE.
28. RECRUIT SEAGULLS.
29. BUY A GIFT.
30. GET A SAWMILL.
31. CALL SOMEONE.
32. WRITE A LETTER.
33. RE-READ A BOOK.
34. GO OUT FOR THE INDOOR SPORTS.
35. DECIDE WHETHER YOU SHOULD OR SHOULDN'T.
36. STAY OUT ALL NIGHT.
37. PLAY THE HORSES.
38. MAKE A DRESS.
39. RESERVE SPACE...

40. CAM
41. LEAR
42. PILOT A SHR
43. TAST
44. SWING
45. LEAD A DISC
46. BUTTE ART UP (per lb)
47. WISH A STAR
48. GET SHANTY
49. BORR PIN ON

MARK WHEELER

152

# HAINES

In 1879 a Presbyterian missionary, S. Hall Young, brought his friend, naturalist John Muir (for whom the Muir Woods just north of San Francisco are named), to see if it might be a good spot to try out the Town-Founding Kit one of them had received for Christmas. They also had brought their credentials as a missionary and a teacher and they tried those out on the Chilkat Indians.

For a name they decided on Haines. Mrs. F. E. Haines was the secretary of the committee of Home Missions but it took them two years to decide to name the place after her.

Haines became an incorporated city in 1910. Its neighbor, Port Chilkoot, always wanting to keep up, incorporated in 1956. In March of 1970 they decided that since they had been living together for so long they may as well get married, so they did. The community is now known as "Haines" (in big letters) and "Port Chilkoot" (in smaller letters).

# WANIGAN

A wanigan is a house or building on a scow which is a barge which is not like in, "Barge right in." Wanigans are a little like floating cabins in which fishermen sometimes play craps which is how floating crap games got started. Now they have been modernized and, along with a new look, they have a new name . . . "Houseboats."

*The Highway from Haines to Anchorage is 785 miles.*

WANiGAN: "WAN" IS ALMOST LIKE "WANT" EXCEPT FOR THE LETTER "T" AND "IGAN" WHICH RHYMES WITH THE CURRENT ALASKA GOVERNOR'S NAME AND WAS USED IN HIS CAMPAIGN SLOGAN, "WE WANIGAN." (REALLY GUV... A GREAT STATE YOU HAVE HERE... LET'S PRESERVE IT!

153

WE NOW PRESENT:

# A BRIEF (BUT NOT SCANTY) HISTORY OF CORDOVA!

1906 - CORDOVA WAS NOT FOUNDED AS CORDOVA BUT AS "EYAK".

1938 - KENNECOTT MINE CLOSED

1963 - FERRY SERVICE STARTED FROM CORDOVA TO VALDEZ AND VICE VERSA.

...SO MUCH FOR HISTORY!

...ALL THAT PLUS LOTS OF OUTDOOR RECREATION AND FUN TOO!:

HUNTING: YOU CAN GO GOATING, DEERING, MOOSING, BEARING, RABBITING, DUCKING, AND GOOSING.

FISHING: YOU CAN GO CATCH A DOLLY VARDEN, RAINBOW, CUTTHROAT, OR A COLD TROUT. FOR SALT WATER FANS, YOU CAN FISH FOR THE SALMON OR FOR THE HALIBUT.

LISTENING: HEAR THE PRINCE WILLIAM SOUND.

...AND NOW A SELECTION OF CORDOVA'S CLAIMS TO FAME, AND WHY:

**"THE RAZOR CLAM CAPITAL OF THE UNIVERSE"**: TO FOLKS FROM IOWA WHO MIGHT NOT KNOW, RAZOR CLAMS SHAVE YOU, THEN YOU EAT THEM.

**"THE FRIENDLY CITY"**: THEY DON'T COME ANY FRIENDLIER THAN CORDOVANS. THE CRACKLING FIREPLACES, THE "OPEN DOOR" POLICY, AND THE SETTING MAKES CORDOVA A "MUST SEE" PLACE IN ALASKA!

**SEE ALSO**: THE ANNUAL **"ICE WORM FESTIVAL"** · FEBRUARY, AND VISIT THE PICNIC PLACES AT LAKE EYAK, OR VISIT COLUMBIA GLACIER, OR VISIT KODIAK SLOUGH, OR VISIT ORCA INLET, OR SEE WHAT'S LEF

＊ CORDOVANS OR CORDUROYS

MARK WHEELER

154

## CORDOVA

Among the things Cordova used to be you can list: Lusty, Rough, Tumble, Old, and Typically Alaskan. Among the things Cordova is today you can list some or all of the above. But you'll have to add, "Growing and Picturesque."

At one time Cordova had a railroad but the word got out that you could send messages by beating on the tracks in Morse Code, and thus save long distance charges. The railroad didn't take too kindly to the practice though and so one day it left town and didn't come back.

The railroad figured if it was going to get treated like that it would get itself, and Cordova, off the beaten track.

Cordova now survives on fishing and all the folks entertain themselves watching the salmon run up and down the Copper River which happens to be in the neighborhood. It is a strange sight to see these salmon running up and down when the much brighter trout swim.

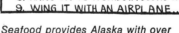

A SELECTED LiST OF WAYS TO GET TO METROPOLiTAN CORDOVA:

1. PADDLE YOUR OWN CANOE...
2. HITCH ONTO A SEAGULL...
3. TAKE THE FERRY FROM VALDEZ...
4. HIKE OVERLAND CAUTIOUSLY...
5. TAKE A SUBMARINE...
6. RIDE ON A SEAL OR WHALE...
7. HITCH YOUR WAGON TO A STAR...
8. HANG ON TO A CORDOVA BOUND MOTH,
9. WING IT WITH AN AIRPLANE...

MARK WHEELER

*Seafood provides Alaska with over $70,000,000 annually.*

YUKON:

FROM: "YOU KONG, ME JANE..."

155

## HOMER

Homer, homey as it is, has a very curious claim to fame. When landlubbers or land-locked folks talk of "spit" they are usually reprimanded by their elders and are told not to expound expletives about expectoration. But when a place needs a handle the place must use that which is most handy.

Homer's spit is an oddity in the landscape which comprises a little finger of land which goes out to sea roughly five miles. Many spits are mostly sand and this one has some too.
If you get a chance to visit Homer you'll find Homerites to be friendly and outgoing folks who love their spit.

*Over half of the State's population works for the federal, state, or local government.*

WHAT HOMER iS PLANNiNG To Do ABOUT iT'S RUCKUS RePUTATiON:

REPUTATIONS DON'T HAPPEN OVERNIGHT NOR DO THEY IMPROVE EASILY. HOMER IS OUT TO CHANGE HERS (OR, IN THIS CASE, HIS) AND HERE IS THE PLAN:

1. BEARS HAVE BEEN RECRUITED TO TRAVEL ALL OVER THE COUNTRY WITH SANDWICH BOARDS PROCLAIMING THE NICETIES OF HOMER...
2. A COORDINATED T.V., RADIO, AND NEWSPAPER CAMPAIGN WILL TOOT ABOUT THE WEATHER AND THE CLIMATE TOO!
3. THE ERRONEOUS RUMOR THAT HOMER DOESN'T EXIST WILL BE QUASHED.
4. THE VISITOR'S BUREAU WILL HAVE ITS BUDGET RAISED BY $7.43.
5. THE C.of C. WILL GET ANOTHER ROLL OF STAMPS.

MARK WHEELER

156

"When we read this brochure back home in Iowa we couldn't imagine why Homer would want to be known for its 'spit'!"

MARK WHEELER

157

MARK WHEELER

"I can't get up!"

158

# TOURISTS

Alaska's population would increase about 50% each year if only the tourists would stay. But apparently the efforts of groups like the P.T.A. (Protect the Animals) and the B.E.A.R.S. (Before Entering Alaska Research Stations) have done much to regulate the length of the tourists' visits.

The average tourist spends close to $425.61 while bouncing around the great land. Of that budget 94% is paid for lodging and breakfast, 4% is for lunch and dinner, 1% goes for hot showers, and that leaves 1% for film, gas, post cards, stamps, moose insurance, payoffs to bears, matches, and mosquito repellents.

Among the favorite sights in Alaska are Mt. McKinley and the animals—at the same time if possible. Also many folks just visit southeastern Alaska and never see Anchorage, Moose Pass, or Bethel, and many Anchorage residents would be tourists if they went to Spenard.

One of the handiest things to have in your luggage is something to pawn. . .

---

The original art for the cartoons in this book is for sale on a first-come first-served basis (naturally). Each will be specially framed and mailed ready to hang. Sizes are:

**Full Pages** (actual size 10″ x 14″)

**Half Page-Verticals** (actual size 7⅞″ x 9⅝″)

**Half Page-Horizontals** (actual size 6¼″ x 13½″)

**Quarter Pages** (actual size 6¼″ x 8″)

Prices upon request.

Please allow four weeks for delivery. All art is subject to prior sale. Orders may be sent to the Publisher:

**Mark Wheeler**
**405 Dock Street**
**Ketchikan, Alaska 99901**

---

159

"MY TALE IS TOLD..."

...ALSO, MY GOOSE MIGHT BE COOKED!

MARK WHEELER

**THE END**

160